CIRCLE OF MYSTERIES

Other Books from Yes International Publishers

Soul Fire: Love Poems in Black and Gold
Alla Renee Bozarth
The Divine Mosaic: Women's Images of the Sacred Other
Theresa King
The Spiral Path: Explorations in Women's Spirituality
Theresa King
Daughters of the Goddess: The Women Saints of India
Linda Johnsen
A Meeting of Mystic Paths: Christianity and Yoga
Justin O'Brien
Walking with a Himalayan Master: An American's Odyssey
Justin O'Brien
The Wellness Tree: A Dynamic Program for Creating Optimal Wellness
Justin O'Brien
Pigs Eat Wolves: Going into Partnership with Your Dark Side
Charles Bates
Ransoming the Mind: An Integration of Yoga and Modern Therapy
Charles Bates
The Yogi: Portraits of Swami Vishnu-devananda
Gopala Krishna
Mirrors: A Journal for Self-Reflection
Cheryl Wall
Mirrors for Men: A Journal for Self-Reflection
Charles Bates & Justin O'Brien

CIRCLE OF MYSTERIES

The Women's Rosary Book

Expanded Edition

°O°O°O°

Christin Lore Weber

Yes International Publishers
Saint Paul, Minnesota

Yes International Publishers
1317 Summit Avenue, St. Paul, MN 55105-2602
Phone: 612-645-6808

Library of Congress Cataloging-in-Publication Data
Weber, Christin Lore
Circle of mysteries : the women's rosary book /
Christin Lore Weber.
--Expanded ed.
p.   cm.
ISBN 0-936663-15-4
1. Women—Prayer-books and devotions—English.
2. Mysteries of the Rosary.
3. Goddess religion.   I. Title.
BL625.7.W44   1997
242'.74—dc21   97-1755
CIP

Printed in the United States of America

To
Aunt Eva
who loved and kept the rosaries

APPRECIATION

I am grateful to the many people whose friendship, faith and creative suggestions inspired this book: to Jan Johnson who conceived the idea and passed it on to me; to Alla R. Bozarth whose poem "We Make God Out of Me: The Song of Mary" first caused me to listen for the voice of Mary in my own soul; to my sister, Liz Kensinger, who gave the book its title. For help in connecting the rosary and its mysteries to Hindu and Jewish tradition I thank Linda Johnsen and Pepe Kahn. And for delivering this book into the world I bless Theresa King who recognized in its mysteries the same spirit I experienced in writing of them.

Thank you to everyone who, through the years, gave me rosaries and believed that I would use them, and to those, particularly my mother, who never ceased their rosary prayer.

Always I thank John whose love makes all my writing possible.

Contents

Part I

My Mother's Beads

My Mother's Beads

Before my mother's mind was lost to Alzheimer's disease, I often found her in the nursing home chapel praying her rosary. She sat in the first chair, second row, most of the time alone, leaning forward slightly, gazing toward the altar. The carved myrtle wood beads of her Jerusalem rosary slipped through her fingers slowly. Her lips moved as if tasting the silent words.

I walked up to her. She didn't notice, lost as she seemed to be in some ancient pleasure. I placed my hand lightly on her shoulder, on the threadbare green sweater that had been my father's, and said in a low voice, "Mama?" She turned her head, embraced me with her smile and said, "Oh, it's you, dear," as if I had been expected, a continuation of her prayer.

Now her Jerusalem rosary hangs on the wall of my office. Each of the beads is a delicate rose lovingly carved by an artist half a world away. Each bead shines, polished by the oils from my mother's fingers as she held it, twirled it around to the rhythm of her prayer, slipped over it to the next and the next, circling through the mysteries of the Mother. The myrtle wood absorbed her prayer as it was polished by her fingers. My mother's prayer is in her beads, and in this room, and in my soul.

Hers is not the only rosary here. Rosaries have been coming to
me, perhaps in an attempt to teach me something. When Sister
Marie Nativity died, Sister Marie Schwan sent me her rosary. It is
a nun's rosary—black and silver, sturdy, shining from constant
use. I have an altar in my office. Sister's rosary is draped over a
large rock from Mt. Shasta under an icon of the young, pregnant
Mary.

Above the altar hangs another rosary, this one a family heirloom. Some years ago, while in Minnesota, I visited my mother's
sister, Eva. "I have something for you," she confided, bustling
into her bedroom. She searched through a carefully organized
drawer filled with little packages. "Ah, here it is!" She pulled out
an old white envelope and handed it to me. On it was written,
"For my niece, Christin Lore Weber."

"I wanted you to have this when I died, but I might as well give
it to you now, then you'll have it for sure. But you have to
promise me one thing. When you die you must leave it to Krista.
Okay?"

"Sure, Aunt Eva." It was a rosary, the most delicate I had ever
seen. Each of the tiny ebony beads is carved into a rose and joined
to the others by an intricate brass chain. The ebony and brass crucifix is less than an inch long. Yet the entire circlet is larger than
most, giving it its particular delicacy.

"This rosary was given to me by my father, your grandfather, on
my confirmation day. His mother brought it from Poland and
gave it to him when he was confirmed. So you see how precious it
is and how it must be passed on."

A year later during my Minnesota visit Aunt Eva produced
another rosary, a bright red and sterling silver circlet. "This was
yours; you gave it to me when you entered the convent. Too pret-
ty for a nun, you said. You'd better have it back, now." I've hung

it on the wall next to the large brass and berry rosary which I wore as part of my habit during my convent years. The hard black berries which form the beads have acquired a burgundy glow polished by praying hands.

I am circled by beads like necklaces around my life. I want more. I want to write to my friends and relatives and beg for rosaries: rosaries stuck away in jewelry boxes, no longer used; rosaries from childhood; rosaries that just turned up, like the intricate sterling silver filigree one I found in a box of memorabilia and must have received as a gift long ago and forgotten; rosaries twined around the fingers of the beloved dead.

I have an instinct about the beads.

I want to enter their mysteries.

Praying the rosary never appealed to me when I was young; I thought the repetition boring. During May and October when our small town parish community of thirty-eight families gathered on Saturday nights to pray the rosary I found the ordeal interminable.

The priest, vested in black cassock and white surplus, came silently out of the sacristy and knelt before the altar. "In the Name of The Father . . . " he droned, beginning the chanting repetitions of prayers that would not release any of us until they had circled through five of the mysteries of our faith. I tried everything to hurry it up. At the beginning of each decade, or group of ten "Hail Marys," the priest announced the mystery. "The first Joyful Mystery..." he paused and then proclaimed, "The Annunciation." I travelled off into a dream of Mary, a tale of

angels and voices in the night. No one ever thought to tell me this
was what I ought to do: think about the event while the prayers
were being said. I figured I was being shrewd. We often finished
with the repetition of the words before my dream of Mary ceased.
The end of the rosary released me by surprise.

While I found the repetition of rosary prayers nearly intolera-
ble, I loved rosaries themselves. I watched fascinated as women
and men fingered their rosaries while waiting for Mass to begin
on Sunday mornings. I liked to match the rosary to the person.
Grandpa Klimek had a brown wooden rosary with beads so worn
that the grain of its light wood could be seen through dark stain.
Just like him: earthy, worn down to the essential, comfortably
familiar. The doctor's wife had crystal beads like diamonds, like
spheres of rainbows. She held her rosary out of bit from the pew
in front of her and seemed to rock while she prayed so that the
glittering beads swung back and forth in a crystal whisper. Most of
the men held black rosaries, but the women's were as multicol-
ored as their personalities: pearl, ivory, silver, ruby, emerald,
lapis, amber, amethyst, carnelian, jasper, topaz, onyx, bloodstone,
rosewood, ebony, oak, laurel, willow, birch, walnut, and myrtle
from Jerusalem. Nearly all the gem beads were glass, I suppose,
but to a child's eyes these rosaries were necklaces of jewels. I
wanted one of rubies. When I was fifteen years old I bought the
chaplet of red glass beads that now hangs near me on my office
wall. It wasn't rubies, but it would suffice.

When I was a young nun in college, Sister Angela and I visited
my family during the Spring break. Angela had a woodworking
class coming up in the next quarter and mentioned to my mother
her desire for some really beautiful wood. Immediately Mama
piled the two of us and my little sister, Betsy, into the car. "A surprise," she explained. We drove out of Baudette on old highway

72 south, and then on a gravel road east through the desolate peat bog. Mama had a liking for wilderness roads. Even a swamp left her undaunted. If we got stuck, she reasoned, we'd just figure a way to get unstuck or, if not, someone would come along—eventually. Angela looked worried as all signs of civilization disappeared and we bumped along the rutted gravel.

In a grove of birch stood a one-room shack. "Well, here we are," Mama announced enthusiastically. "Old Jake's."

"Who's old Jake?" I inquired.

"Diamond Willow," she replied.

The old man came out to meet us, pipe in his teeth, weight supported by a gnarled, lustrous walking stick—a finely worked, waxed, buffed diamond willow cane.

"It washes up from the islands," Old Jake explained as he showed us the piles of wood he had collected, "cured by the lake water and the sun, hard as diamond. But its the knotholes gives it the name. Shaped like diamond and just as brilliant when you polish 'em."

Jake made canes for sale. That was how Mama met the old man. She saw him peddling diamond willow canes up and down the streets of Baudette one Saturday afternoon during tourist season. She had an eye for the unique and beautiful. Now she bought diamond willow for Angela.

Angela made a rosary. She carved each bead. Diamond of the willow for the end-place where the crucifix would be on most chaplets. In the center of the diamond, a thorn shaped like a cross. Waxed and knotted twine joined the beads. Angela made a rosary from the wood of the island trees, broken by storms, washed out onto the lake, drifted ashore, cured by the sun, found by the hermit of the bog, seen by my mother as beautiful. Angela took fragments of the earth, collected them, and made them whole. With a bit of twine Angela made a circle of earth. Angela made a diamond willow rosary.

Now, in the middle of my life, I am lured by circlets of beads. What I never understood when young, now I am being drawn to appreciate. What once seemed to be the boring devotion of simple folks, now begins to be revealed as the mysticism of the wise. There are secrets in these beads, women's secrets preserved over the centuries in the mystic necklace, in the chaplet, in the circle of the rose. I am compelled by the allurement of the beads to open myself to the secrets, now linked together in the Mother's chaplet, a circle of mysteries.

Rosary Beginnings

I begin. I take beads of olive wood from Jerusalem. Marya, my eighty-some-year-old Jewish friend, gave them to me as a necklace. "These are like you," she said as she pressed them into my open hand. Her accent is New York. Her family brought her here as an infant from the Soviet Union, Russia, during the persecutions. Others, family friends and relatives, escaped to Israel. She visits there. She's been a world traveler; she also gave me a silk kimono from Singapore; but Israel is as much her home as are the Contra Costa County hills of California.

I smile as I slip the beads off the simple cotton string. Some are plain. Others, larger ones, are carved with concentric circles, symbol of the unending, of completion, and reminiscent of the rose. I plan to make a rosary for my sister, Liz. A sense of the links between women is in my fingers as I work. We are linked across cultures and religious beliefs. We are intertwined by family, friendship, and the mysteries of joy, sorrow, and glory that suffuse our lives. I knot the twine between beads. Even time and death are not enough to separate us.

Who was the first woman to fashion beads into a circle? I wonder as I work. Was it when the beads slipped through her fingers, maybe as she counted them to balance the design, that she felt a calming effect? Did she think of it as magic? Entrancement? When did someone associate this experience with sacred realities and begin to use the beads in prayer?

I know that rosaries didn't originate with Catholic Christians. Hindus of India have used the *japa mala*, a string of beads, or more literally, seeds, in their worship since long before the birth of Jesus. A different variety of seed ordinarily is used in the worship of a specific form of the divine. Devotees who worship the divine in the form of Lord Shiva or the Divine Mother often use rudaraksha seeds in their *mala* which are believed to be "the tears of Shiva." Those who worship Vishnu use *malas* fashioned of tulasi or lotus seeds, or even fragrant beads carved from sandalwood. The wealthy sometimes incorporate gems and crystals into their *malas*.

Even though all forms of the deity are worshipped with the *mala*, the Goddess of Wisdom, Sarasvati, is most closely associated with this circle of prayer beads. With her four hands Sarasvati holds a *vina* (a precursor to the modern sitar; she is matron of musicians), a book (she is also matron deity of scholars and students), and a rosary or *mala* (revealing her role as source of divine inspiration to those engaged in religious practice).[1]

Now my fingers slide over the beads. I choose the larger, carved beads to place at the beginning of each of five mysteries in the circle. As a child I learned that the rosary came into our Roman Catholic religious tradition through St. Dominic. As he knelt in the Church of St. Sabina in Rome, Mary, the Queen of Heaven, is said to have appeared and given him a rosary, asking him to spread devotion to her through the prayer of the beads.

However, the Christians of Europe had kept and prayed with rosaries for centuries before St. Dominic's time. Historians now believe that rosaries may have come into Christianity through the Crusades, brought by the crusaders into Europe from the Moslems, who probably acquired the prayer beads from the Hindus.

It could also be that the rosary practice arose spontaneously in the West as well as in the East. Marina Warner, in her classic work on *Mary, Alone of All Her Sex,* mentions that "In 1014, Lady Godiva of Coventry left in her will a circlet of gems on which she used to say her prayers."[2] This rosary predated the crusades.

Maybe stringing beads, experiencing them slip through our fingers and turning the experience into prayer is a natural thing, more basic to us than the distinctions our various religious traditions create. While I string the Jerusalem beads for my sister I sort through the images I associate with rosaries now, in the middle of my life.

For me the rosary is a holy object that connects me to my origin, and the origin of all creation. We spring from God's womb, the Mother-Womb of the Holy One. In art this divine womb is pictured as the cosmic rose. The rosary, in Western spirituality, is what has survived of our devotion to the motherhood of God. It is the mother-prayer. The feminine principle in God has been called by many names: Great Rose, Mother of All, Flower of Venus, Rose of Divine Love. The "World Tree" of the East was a rose-tree. Barbara Walker tells us this was a female tree of life and immortality and that in Central Asia it was called Woman, the Wellspring.[3]

Rose windows in Gothic cathedrals were dedicated to Mary, the

Mystical Rose. In Mary, Christian Europeans of the Gothic era honored what we now call images of the divine feminine: the Great Mother, the World Tree, the Rose Garden, the Mother-Womb of the World, the Cosmic Rose. All these images found expression in Gothic architecture, especially in the mandala-like rose window.

I do not forget, either, that Mary was a simple Jewish woman in an ancient Israel then occupied by the foreign power, Rome. As I work with Marya's Jerusalem beads, I imagine Mary engaged in ordinary tasks: weaving, going to the village well, cooking, playing with her boy, maybe even stringing beads. She lived the mysteries, as each of us does, in a cultural context at a specific historical time. The Christian mysteries I live today spring from the land, the soul, the rich traditions of the Jews. The rosary is the rose garland of the mother's mysteries. Marina Warner reflects that "the beads are actively holy in themselves, and are often lovingly carved and jewelled and numbered among a person's most treasured possessions. . . . In the rosary, the use of incantatory prayers blended with the medieval symbolism of the rose until the beads themselves were seen to be chaplets to crown the queen of heaven, as garlands for the rose without thorn (Ecclesiasticus 23:14), the rose of Sharon (Song of Solomon 2:1), the rose of Jericho, the rose in which the Word became flesh, as Dante wrote, which flowers at the center of the arrayed petals of the mystic rose in the empyrean (Paradiso 23)."[4]

Christian people around the world claim to experience visions in which the rosary is given as a means of accessing divine mysteries. Mary keeps appearing to people and giving them rosaries! When I was young I took these apparitions literally. I yearned to see as Bernadette, the peasant girl from Lourdes, could see. I wanted the sun to whirl for me as it did for the shepherd children of Fatima.

At this time in my life I want a wider faith, not limited by literalism. But I do wonder, as I have always wondered, what is happening there, where the people claim to see her. I know that the mystic, philosopher, psychologist Carl G. Jung interpreted the visitation of Mary at Lourdes as the appearance of the archetypal feminine arising from the depths of the collective unconscious to proclaim herself good: "I am the Immaculate Conception!"

Some years ago, I had lunch with a woman I met by coincidence. She heard from a friend that I might be writing a book on the rosary. She was interested. "Do you realize," she said as she leaned toward me over the cafe table and locked onto me with her intense blue eyes, "that Mary appears in places sacred to the Goddess? In France where the Paleolithic statue of Venus was found in the Grotte du Pappe, Mary appeared in a grotto of rock to St. Bernadette. And now, in Medjugorje, so close to the site of the ancient Catal Huyuk, where the worship of the Goddess in the West is thought to originate, she's appearing again. I think the ancient Goddess is making herself known in a way we will accept, in the image of Mary."

We speak in symbols, in metaphors. We speak of the mysteries where human meets divine; how can we speak in any other way? Perhaps we've reached a time when the divine feminine is bursting forth in us, rising, proclaiming her presence. Perhaps what we see is what is within us. Perhaps what is proclaimed through visions is the presence of the divine essence in everything.

Visions of the divine feminine rise in us and are seen however we can see her, however our culture and belief systems permit. Perhaps her mysteries are what is divine in creation, that which we experience in our depth. Perhaps the divine feminine, beyond her many names and faces, is that aspect of the one God which is the center, the womb, the rose.

All images of God are, of course, metaphorical communications of unknowable mystery fashioned in a language we creatures can take in and accept. God transcends gender, but we do not. In our sexuality we experience what is deepest in life: love, conception, birth, lactation, and the wise blood of menopause which initiates the passage to death. We seek to understand the mystery of God in the only way we can, through the deepest experiences we have. Images of God which include both men's and women's experience of the mystery are the only images that are whole.

I tie the last knot in my sister's rosary and admire what I have made. She'll slip the beads through her fingers while she prays the prayer of her heart. In a year or two the beads will shine from the oils in her skin. Marya, who brought them from Jerusalem, will be blessed by my sister's prayer. I, too, will experience blessing. Together my sister and I will enter the mysteries by way of these circles of beads. We follow our mother's path.

Many women today are entering the mystery and telling their visions. This is a courageous undertaking because to do it we must believe in ourselves. No one can tell us what to see. The visions are within us.

Mary, the mother of Jesus, is one of us. Her mysteries are ours. They are as common as ours and as profound. They are made of earth and are the gateway into the holy.

The old woman in the chapel knew. My mother knew. Before she died she wore her beads around her neck; she didn't want to lose them; she lost many things those days but the rosary was essential. She slipped it over her head and fingered the beads. These are the fragments of women's lives. The beads. The task is to make a circlet, a necklace of roses, a wholeness of woman's wisdom. And it has been done. The feeling of the beads comforts even when there is no prayer. They are the mother's beads. She is the Mystical Rose. She is present here and waiting.

It is my turn now. I pick up my mother's beads. I enter the mysteries.

The Rosary Prayer

I unwittingly discovered the essence of the rosary prayer when I was just a child and imagined events in the lives of Jesus and Mary rather than making myself concentrate on the words of the "Hail Mary" prayer which I was reciting. The rosary prayer is a form of meditation.

I hold the rosary. It's designed into five groups of ten beads with each group separated by a single bead set off from the rest. Where the five groups of beads connect there is often a silver medal with an image of Mary on one side and Jesus on the other. From this hang another five beads, grouped so that the three beads in the center are separated from those on each end. The rosary is completed by a crucifix.

The entire rosary consists of fifteen meditations and a full rosary actually has fifteen sets of ten beads. But most people use the smaller rosary, also called a chaplet. Ordinarily people pray one chaplet of the rosary on a given day. The chaplet consists of five meditations, each of which focuses on a particular Christian mystery. On Mondays and Thursdays one meditates on joyful mysteries, the sorrowful mysteries on Tuesdays and Fridays, and glorious mysteries on Wednesdays and Saturdays. On Sundays the mysteries coincide with the season: joyful mysteries during the Advent and Christmas, sorrowful mysteries during Lent, and glorious mysteries from Easter on throughout the reminder of the year.

I begin the rosary prayer while holding the crucifix, the symbol of Christ's death and resurrection. This is the doorway into the mysteries, the opening of my heart in faith. My fingers slip onto the first bead. The words of Jesus's prayer, "The Our Father," take form in my mind. This prayer is endless, it's depth as infinite as God. I let it take me. Sometimes one phrase, sometimes another holds me. God is All. This prayer to the Father balances the Mother imagery to come. My fingers find the three small beads: I think of all the threes—faith, hope and charity; virgin, mother, crone; creator, redeemer, sanctifier—as they come to me. I rest in the grace of God. The path this meditation takes depends upon the spirit, the Mother of mysteries, the wisdom of God. I hear the words of the "Hail Mary," the words the angel sang, words recorded in the Gospel of Luke. Three times these words repeat themselves in my heart. My fingers caress the beads. A single bead, then, and the Glory prayer: "Glory be to the Father and to the Son and to the Holy Spirit; as it was in the beginning, is now and ever shall be. Amen." This mystery is fathomless.

Now the circle. My fingers hold the image of Mary and Jesus. The first of the mysteries surfaces in my mind. "The Annunciation." I follow the beads around the circle. For each mystery my mind says the words of one Our Father, ten Hail Marys and one Glory prayer. As I repeat the words of the prayers I let the beads slip through my fingers. It is a way of counting without needing to think about it. The words of the prayers are, themselves, a way of focusing without thinking. They are repetitive, trance-inducing, prayers through which I sink into deep meditation on the mysteries.

Each chaplet of mysteries is a meditation on either joy, sorrow or glory that can, if I allow it, transform my life. I can enter into the mysteries at any depth. I might imagine the story recalled by the mystery. For example, in the first joyful mystery of the "Annunciation" I can visualize the Angel Gabriel appearing to the young girl, Mary, in her home at Nazareth and asking her to be the mother of God. At another level I might personalize this mystery, reflecting on my own responses to the call of God, the appearance in my own life of what might be called angels. More deeply still I might actually become the mystery while I pray it, listening for the voice of God's angel in the moment and responding as I pray. Finally I might experience that each mystery is the essence of my deepest self. I am the mysteries.

Each of the rosary mysteries comes from the scriptures and traditions of Christianity. Many of them are grounded in the historical life of Jesus and his mother. All of them are focal points of human life. Any one of them, lived, is a divine path into the fullness of God.

THE JOYFUL MYSTERIES

1. The Annunciation: The angel Gabriel appears to Mary and she conceives by the Holy Spirit, becoming pregnant with the Son of God, whom we call Jesus.
2. The Visitation: Mary visits her elder cousin, Elizabeth, who is miraculously pregnant with John the Baptist. Both women are filled with the gift of prophecy.
3. The Nativity: Jesus is born.
4. The Presentation of Jesus in the Temple and the Purification of Mary: Jesus and Mary take their place in the history of salvation. Jesus is proclaimed "Light to the Gentiles."

5. The Finding of Jesus in the Temple: Jesus proclaims his identity as Son of God.

THE SORROWFUL MYSTERIES

1. The Agony in the Garden: Jesus confronts the fear of death and accepts the will of God.
2. The Scourging at the Pillar: Jesus endures torture and is stripped of every vestige of humanity.
3. The Crowning with Thorns: Jesus's divine kingship is mocked.
4. The Carrying of the Cross: Jesus bears the burden of all our pain.
5. The Crucifixion and death of Jesus.

THE GLORIOUS MYSTERIES

1. The Resurrection: Jesus is raised from death.
2. The Ascension: Jesus ascends to heaven.
3. The Descent of the Holy Spirit: The Spirit of God enters Mary and the apostles bringing gifts of wisdom, understanding, counsel, fortitude, knowledge, piety and awe in the presence of God.
4. The Assumption: Mary, at her death, joins her son in heaven.
5. The Coronation of Mary: Mary is proclaimed the queen of heaven and earth.

The meditations that rise from the rosary prayer today will be as varied as those who pray. One group of people who might well pick up a chaplet and enter the mysteries are those who have glimpsed the feminine face of God. Meditation in the presence of this feminine face of God gives added dimension to the rosary mysteries. A woman's meditation might take this form:

MYSTERIES OF JOY (Women experiencing paradox)

1. The Annunciation: The mystery of the call of divine love. Claiming of personal identity as basic to women's creativity.

2. The Visitation: The mystery of the Mother dancing the world into being. Inter-connection is woman's prophecy.

3. The Nativity: The mystery of birth. The world is our child. There are many forms of mothering.

4. The Presentation and the Purification: The mystery of release. Letting go creates the emptiness needed for new creation.

5. The Finding of Jesus in the Temple: The mystery of love's infinite presence. In our experiences of loss we find the fullness of life within.

MYSTERIES OF SORROW (Women experiencing transformation)

1. The Agony in the Garden: The mystery of fear. We transform the death of our dreams.

2. The Scourging at the Pillar: The mystery of emptiness. We transform violence, abuse, and the desecration of beauty.

3. The Crowning with Thorns: The mystery of despair. We transform social systems and the abuse of power.

4. The Carrying of the Cross: The mystery of unknowing. We transform the masculine within ourselves and in our sons.

5. The Crucifixion: The mystery of death. We are transformed by death and all that overwhelms us.

THE MYSTERIES OF GLORY (Women experiencing compassionate wholeness)

1. The Resurrection: The mystery of the open heart. We speak the language of a transformed life by communicating in the mother tongue: simple, subtle, loving.

2. The Ascension: The mystery of universal connections. We
   unite the opposites in ourselves and in the world—male and
   female, earth and heaven, the human and divine, Yahweh and
   Shekhinah.
3. The Descent of the Holy Spirit: The mystery of the spiritualiza-
   tion of matter. The one God with many names is whole in
   each of us. The spirit frees God's gifts into the world through
   our lives.
4. The Assumption of Mary: The mystery of the Mother's return.
   All that we've rejected in our lives, now we can embrace. We
   are whole.
5. The Coronation of Mary: The mystery of divine love as the
   Mother. Divine wisdom is love, is the original one. In wisdom
   all creation is whole. Creation wears the crown of God.

Wisdom spoke the first word into the human heart and awakened our consciousness of being. She is the original one. The
Mother. She holds us in her divine womb. Nothing exists outside
her circle and she fills everything that is. We called her that as
soon as we could speak: Mother, the one who is all and who is in
all and contains all. She calls us to approach her, to remember
her, to fill ourselves with her, to inherit her. And it is time. At last
we return to her claiming our inheritance.

The mystery that we have called so many different names
depending on when we have lived and where, throughout the history and in the cultures of this world, transcends all names. We
cannot name what we cannot comprehend. Every name distorts
the reality of the Holy One by circumscription. When we name,
we do so for our own benefit, out of our own need to respond to
the summons of incomprehensible and ultimate life and love. In
our present times we need to remember the Mother's name and

cry it out in response to an ever increasing divine call articulated in the language of every being. Hers is the name we need to speak today in order to survive. Her name is not so much a word as an activity. Our response to her summons is a coming out to meet the mystery of life in every moment and in everything. The meeting is the prayer of creation, the worship inherent in our coming-to-be.

To the question, Is Mary the same as the feminine face of God, is she the Divine Mother? the answer is yes and no. Mary is a way that we have known her who is, herself, a construct of our own minds and hearts, an image to assist our response to the mystery we sometimes vaguely, sometimes keenly sense within and surrounding everything-that-is. Mary is but one name and face she wears. There are many. Each name, each face represents an aspect of the call we hear and the response we give.

She is also the response. Hers is the name for the infinite intimacy of the Holy One. Hers is an intimacy so total that She actually becomes our response to the ultimate mystery of being. This attribute is what makes Her so vital to our times. She is the body of the holy and that body is ours. Her womb incarnates the divine Word. When we love the body of the world, when we honor and preserve the land and all her creatures, when we reach out our hands to heal and nourish, when we break bonds of oppression and do the work of justice responding to the summons in our deepest heart, then we call her by name in an act of faith that can restore creation and renew the face of the earth.

Mary is a human, womanface of wisdom, the Sophia of God, the queen of heaven and earth. Her queenship is the mystery of our remembering, in its fullness, in its glory. This is the mystery of restoration, not only of the Godwomb with the Godhead, but of women to full partnership in the work and play of creation.

This is her crowning and it is ours. Her crown is not the crown of kings. Hers is the circlet. Her crown is nature, the circle of cosmos, the spiral of being. She assumes no power over anyone or anything. She represents our power of life itself. We are her crown. She is crowned in every circle that we make. Circles of women. Circles of our children at play. Healing circles. Dancing circles. Circles of governance and the making of decisions. Birthing circles. Circles around the dying. Circles around war camps where we sing songs and perform acts of courage to save the earth. A circle of beads, a necklace we slip through our fingers remembering her, remembering ourselves from the beginning and through many ends. A shining circlet of glorious rememberings. A rosary of stars. A cosmic crown.

This is a book for meditating on the rosary as it reveals to us this feminine face of God. In each mystery we present ourselves to wisdom, the Divine Mother. We lay our hearts open to her and she responds. Then we look at Mary. She also laid her heart open. She also was one of us who let wisdom, the Sophia of God, enter her soul and her mind. She let wisdom take flesh in her womb and be born a man. We listen to this woman who was so like us. We see how much her life was transformed.

PART II

THE WOMEN'S ROSARY MEDITATIONS

I Believe

In my hand I hold the cross.

I look deep into my soul.

I search for what I believe.

Mary Speaks

What has been my secret from the beginning, now I reveal. My vision I proclaim in a Word that is planted in my womb, in my eyes, in my mind, in my hands that knead the bread and spin the threads of life. My own mother whispered in my ear, when I was still a girl winding roses for a garland to hang around her neck, "What you have heard is true, Mary. It is God's gift."

I feel the holy in my bones and in pebbles rounded by rain and piled in the hills where the sand mouse makes her nest. Ruah, God who is breath, moves the sky bringing clouds to cool the afternoon earth, to cool my wet face; I lift myself to the caress and receive her into my own heart remembering I am the breath of God enfleshed.

One eternal love, source and center of the world, Creator, I proclaim you.

The universe enfleshes you and is your child and all is one eternal love.

I am that child, as is the child who comes from me, and all that is born and comes to consciousness of you—we are the universe, one love enfleshed, one body flung forth in being, whirling into you in a return that is eternal. I see it everywhere. In the cycles of my blood. In the moon and in the seasons of the stars, the seasons of the earth, the seasons moving every creature's life.

I proclaim Sophia, wisdom spirit, dance of love, music of the stars, fire of becoming, who, from the center which is everywhere, expands our consciousness of being.

I respect the mystery of pain. I accept the humbling of mind when sons and daughters die without reason, against all hope; when the world seems prodigal with life in fires and floods and the heat scorching the fields leaving us hungry.

I mourn the evil that divides the world, the lie that seeks to destroy the one eternal love, the domination that unleashes war, the senselessness that turns us against our one body, that leaves us blind and without heart.

This I know:

The world will rise through evil and through pain and be born anew in one eternal love, over and over, like the seasons, as often as it takes until creation is the perfect body of God.

Nothing is lost. All is present and alive in love.

Wrongs are forgiven and evil can and will be transformed into power for life.

Everything created lives forever in the one eternal love.

Mother Wisdom Speaks

I am the maiden of joy.

I am song in the wind and rain upon the rocks. I am fair love and
holy hope and the flight of the dove. I am earth, betrothed. I
am mystical rose.

I am the Mother of mystery.

I hold opposites together. I birth children and sever the cord with
my teeth. Those I love I send away to their lives. I am the caul-
dron of fire and the cup of milk. I am the two-edged knife.

I am the old woman: I am the queen.

If you seek me you will find me everywhere. I am the womb of
wise blood. I am the world's crown. I am diamond. I am pearl.
I shine with the wisdom of God.

I am the circle of being.

I am glory—splendor of infinite life. I am the spiral, the fullness
of being, fully becoming, forever, world without end.

MYSTERIES OF JOY

Teach me joy

The paradox

That in my emptiness

I am most whole

I placed a snapshot of my mother in a rose-colored leather frame, one that shuts like a locket, but is the size of a small book. Rose velvet lines the cover opposite her. She is young. Wind sweeps her hair back from her face and lifts the collar of her white cotton blouse. Behind her the leaves of oak trees are etched lacy against a summer sky. She is smiling into the sun. To me she is beautiful.

It was the summer of her joy. But like all joy it dawned in her at the breathtaking and sheer edges of being where life is fragile and uncertain. Paging through the photo album with me when I was a child she told such stories! Arriving at this picture she nearly always sighed, touched it lightly, nostalgically and said, "I was so happy that summer. Just to be outside! Look, there, at the wind—you can see it in my hair. For a year I didn't feel the wind," she laughed, remembering. "My poor Mom. She could hardly keep me down. They told her she must try or I could have a relapse of the TB, and she did try, really. But the summer felt so delicious! The grass between my toes. Breathing the air; breathing and not coughing. It was joy, Sweetie, pure joy."

Irony. This is what we know of joy. She could have died. Joy is seldom pure. It surprises us, even in our pain. During life on earth we discover joy in paradox.

"Follow your bliss," counsels Joseph Campbell in the nearly

mystical interviews he gave Bill Moyers just before the great mythologist's death. "Yes!" I concurred, "Yes, yes!" Such a simple rule for life. I told a friend. She stared at me, puzzled. "But how do I know," she replied slowly, "what my bliss is?"

Each joyful mystery asks us, What is joy?

Each of Mary's mysteries of joy involves a paradox. Before I grasped the paradoxical nature of joy these mysteries troubled me. Each of them seemed joyful only on the surface while just underneath hid something troublesome. The angel's announcement of Mary's destiny as Mother of God and her acceptance of pregnancy put her in danger of death by stoning. The law of Moses would have judged her guilty of adultery.

The meeting between the pregnant cousins, Mary and Elizabeth, released in each of them the spirit of prophecy, a dubious gift in a nation with a history of rejecting its prophets.

The joy of birth always implies some kind of death for a woman; it might be simply death of the life and personality she had before motherhood; it might be, and often was in Mary's time, literal death of the mother or the child or both. This birth of Mary's boy took place on a journey, under the poorest of conditions, as the parents fulfilled the decree of a foreign power in a tiny country enduring the throes of political occupation. From the beginning Mary's son was threatened by those who wanted him dead.

When Mary and Joseph presented Jesus in the Temple of Yahweh, Simeon and Anna predicted the child's paradoxical destiny and warned Mary of the sword forged to pierce her heart.

Finally, Mary's joy in finding the lost Jesus in the Temple seems overshadowed by the boy's enigmatic response to his parents' understandable anxiety. Here Mary did what most women finally do with the mystery of life: she kept all these things, pondering them in her heart.

In the Mother's mysteries all the opposites are joined. The dualities of life are not only at opposite ends of a continuum, they are joined in a circle, they are a sphere, light and dark as the moon, changing in degrees of fullness every day. Yet both light and darkness remain in balance, essential to the other, completing the other.

Joy results from surrender to this mystery of paradox, the mystery of the maiden-mother.

Hers are the five mysteries of creation. They reveal the phases of creation in story form. Conception, recognition, birth or creation, and surrender of one's child, first to the mystery and then to the child's destiny. Five is a number designating the presence of women's mysteries. Five petals of the wild rose. Five points in the star at the core of the apple representing woman's fruitful sexuality.

As I write this John, my spouse, brings me two red roses from his garden, one full blown, one a delicate bud. "I love you," he smiles. Joy enlarges my heart. I place them by the picture of my mother in the summer of her joy. I am vaguely aware as I continue to write that this is May, Mary's month. Not long ago the earth women celebrated Beltane. Tomorrow, Pentecost Sunday, combines with Mother's Day. All these observances are connected somehow with the roses and a picture of a very young woman with shining eyes whom I never knew for she lived before I was born. She smiles out at me from the summer of her joy, at the time of her annunciation when her angel whispered her name on the wind.

"Alyce," my mother's angel came in flames of sunlight on the wind, "Alyce Rose. Live and be fruitful."

THE VOICE OF AN ANGEL

THE FIRST JOYFUL MYSTERY

THE ANNUNCIATION

°O°○°O°

The Woman Speaks

Mother of mysteries, when I was a child I heard the voice of my angel. She sang to me in wind through cottonwood trees, a sound like water rushing over rocks. She sang with the voice of lake water shivering in a sudden summer breeze, catching sunlight, becoming a shimmer of stars. She sang at the moment of dawn and was the last song I heard at night, a murmur of crickets and frogs. I heard her in my mother's lullaby, and felt her in my father's tender strength. While I slept she stood like a pillar of light at the bottom right-hand corner of my bed so I would never be alone.

My angel sang from my terror, too. When I awoke into the deep and frightening dark, when I screamed through a nightmare so real I could not dispel it by the strength of my own reason, she was there. She came in the soft body of my mother, in the tears which released the clutching of monsters at my soul, in the urging to believe that I was brave and more real than the terrible images crowding in my dreams. She was the warm breath of the mother on my face, the mother able to sleep, trusting sleep, trusting the deep darkness, surrendering to dreams, drawing me with her into a sweet calm.

She sang from everywhere and when she sang I heard her call my name.

Are you the song my angel sang?

Mother Wisdom Speaks

I have always been.
There is not time that I did not come forth.
I am the song.
I am the endless opening, the infinite widening of the Godhead.
I am the Word from the everlasting breath.
I am the sound originating in eternal silence.
I am love.

I am who calls from every cell, every atom.
I erupt in mountains, I am fire.
I am the circle, the spiral of reality.
I am the universe and I always return to the holy.
I am the green of grass and trees, the red of the rose, the gold of
   dawn.
I am the blue of the playing waves.
I am the dance of stars.
I am the fire in your heart.
I am your longing.
I am the one and the many becoming one.

I am the simple woman, the mother nourishing the child.
I am her flesh.
I am the eyes that heal.
I am the hands that smooth away fears.
I am the smile that consoles.

I am the divine.

There is nothing in you where I am not.
I am the ringing in your voice, the light of your truth, the calming
of your fear.
I am what is smallest in your gestures of kindness and I am the
kindness itself.
I am the hug of infinite tenderness.

Come to me all you who desire me.
Come and be filled.
I am the breast, the fountain, the eternal river of compassion.
I love you and I am you.
I am both your center and all you will become.
I am your outgoing; I am your within.
I am your joy.
I am what turns you into air, what dissolves the hardness of your
heart, what melts your fear.
I call and you reach out to me.
You will never be alone.
You will never be alone.
You will never be alone.

Come then. Open your heart to me.
I am all you've ever known or wanted to know.
I am all you've ever loved.
Come to me.

I will take you to the holy, I will take you to the heart of God.
I am so much more than you have imagined.
I am beyond your widest mind.

I am beyond your hopes.
Be wide.
Be endless.
My gifts to you are without limit.
My hope for you knows no end.
I will take you to God.
I will take you to the one, to the wholeness, to the complete love.

Mary Speaks

Abba. You spoke your name in me one night when I was three and lay crying on my sleeping pallet. I saw shapes of evil in the dark. Old Joachim heard my sobs and, careful not to awaken my mother, rose, lit the lamp, and came to my side. He sang. My father sat cross-legged on the floor and sang to me of you.

In the song my father sang you made yourself known to me. You lifted me up with your strength and filled me with your light until I could no longer remember my fear. No one told me but you, yourself. They told me you are Yahweh, you are Adonai, you are Elohim, you are the mighty and the powerful. But when I was three years old I curled into the song my father sang and fell asleep in your arms as you whispered your name to me—Abba, tender Father, Father of gentle hands, Father of the soft voice, Father who hears me in the night and sings my fear away, Father whose compassion kisses away my tears and whose strength is love.

°O°○°O°

I am whole within myself. I never tear my soul in two; I make love, but I will never relinquish my name. I keep my truth and bear my womanhood intact. I love the passage into my depths and allow only love to journey there. The world wants to be born from me. Only the virgin soul conceives God; only the virgin is whole enough. Love never divides. My virginity cannot be lost except by the denial of my destiny or the relinquishment of my name.

She folded round me with wings softer than breath and whispered every secret of my heart. I knew her. She showed me my soul in the mirror of God. When she spoke her voice was the perfection of my own. Her word was who I am. I recognized her immediately. No one had to tell me. No one could prove her presence or her truth. I knew it. What she said to me was natural as blood, natural as my laughter, natural as my tears. No one needed to say to me, "do this," or "you ought." I have listened to my angel. Now I do what I am.

I am trembling. I fear my yes. I fear myself. I did not know that I could bear such power or be such blessed beauty. I am but a girl not far beyond my first blood, newly woman, not yet wise. I don't want to die. I want to run carefree to the hills and to the little stream where bees gather in wild roses; I want to stand naked in clear water and wash my hair with chamomile and let it dry in the sun. I want to feel the silk of my hair over my breasts where I stand alone in the dry, hot breeze of Galilee. I want my life. I want my simple self.

I am more than I am. I am the bee and the breeze, the stream and the blossom on the wild rose. I am the round, full earth. I bow before a mystery. How can this be? I am more than clay containing God's breath. I am the body of the earth, all life comes from me. I am the multiplicity of being. I am the morning star. I am Hannah cradling her son. I am she who comes forth from the sea. I am she who is becoming. I am every woman. I bow down; I touch my head to the earth; I am filled with awe. I am the Mother.

°O°O°O°

Your words, Angel, contradict all that I have ever learned. How can this be? Who is it that you think I am? What you proclaim religion will call blasphemy: God does not have a son according to its law, the Lord our God is one. If I say yes to you will I become the mother of idolatry? Will I be outcast? Will I be stoned by the fathers in the village square? This is not legitimate. Can I conceive what is so disapproved? Have you spoken with the priest? Does this proposal circumvent the law? If I say yes won't this change the order of the world?

°O°O°O°

Ruah, rush of wings, breath, shadow of the holy, immediate calm, I have never been so still. This is the marriage of wisdom with the sacred earth; she who danced the world into being now dances in my heart and speaks her word into my womb. The

questions dissolve. Fear melts like the mists of morning. I stand in
the light. I am graciousness. I am the smile of wisdom. I am the
mother of God. I step lightly with the breeze and lift my veil. I
begin the dance.

This time of year the hills are green from the winter rains and
everywhere wild flowers splendor the earth. Nothing is barren. I
will go to Elizabeth, the house of God. I will go to Elizabeth who
is my cousin, my sister, any woman. Over the springtime hills I
will go to my beloved Elizabeth who was barren but will now give
birth. No one need ever be barren again. Each woman's gift can
now be conceived and brought into the world. Woman is the
house of God. I will go to Elizabeth. Together we will deliver her
child. Nothing can stop us.

The lark does not resist her song but ascends singing towards
the sun. It does not make her proud to sing and soar that way;
song is her delight and the sky her being. Now I live each
moment like the lark at dawn. I fly. I sing. I live my self. If I die
so living I will have died complete. I have listened to my angel;
now I know my name. I am Mary-Full-of-Grace.

The holy is within. Within is everywhere. Within is all. I have
heard the voice of God in trees and in the little rocks that line the
shore of the Lake of Galilee. The Word came whirling from the

midsummer night's stars and settled on me where I stood in our lady moon's white shimmering. I brought wisdom up in water from the village well, cool on the lips of old Anna, at noon on a weary desert day. I recognized compassion in my hands the night that Sarah came with tears to tell me of her spouse's death and I touched her face, blessed her with her tears and took her in my arms. I feel the resonance of God connecting everything. My own heart feels when God is here. What is not of God divides. The Word my angel spoke connects heaven and earth. That Word is God. To God alone I will surrender my life.

The Holy One is planted in my womb, in my mind, in my heart, in the vast openness of my woman-being. What will emerge could be a child, a poem, a loaf of bread, a healing touch, a creative idea, a garden, a whole new world. I am gentle as a rose closing around dew. This God in me is but a flutter of difference, a barely perceptible change, secret as the first whisper of love. I wrap myself around the seed of the holy. I wait. I work the magic of my womanhood. This seed will grow.

Glory to the Word, the voice of the holy, the whisper of wisdom where I have been large, and round, and empty as the ocean or the sky. Glory where life bursts forth from thought, from seed, from everything and all. Glory to the completeness of God within and around me world without end. Amen.

THE DANCING SONG

THE SECOND JOYFUL MYSTERY

THE VISITATION

The Woman Speaks

Mother of mysteries, women live in me. I feel my sister in myself, sinewy, something in my flesh, in my heart cells, in the texture of my skin and the timbre of my voice. Her hand, when she places it in mine, is as familiar as my own. She runs across the hills to me. I hear her greet me with the recognition of the secrets I contain, the secrets I will spin into words and weave into manuscripts. I greet her back, understanding that what she contains is for a future I will never know. I love her secrets. I rejoice in her becoming, in her conceptions, in the children of womb, of mind, of heart she will bring to birth, children beyond my dreams.

I feel we are a prophecy. We prophecy from our wombs, from the center of creativity. We believe the word that is spoken in us. We cry it out. We sing. We dance.

We need to open our doors to one another. We need to open our eyes to one another. We need to become sensitive to the stirrings in our wombs—our centers of creativity. We need to be moved by the creative spirits of one another. We need to embrace one another until the circle we make and the dance we create embraces the world.

Mother of mysteries, be our meeting and our dancing song.

Mother Wisdom Speaks

I am the swinging of hips; I am the dance.
Do you feel the fire?
Do you hear the word?
Do not be afraid to move, to jump, to fly, to twirl.

Let your hair grow long.
Let your hair sing out like clouds across the sky, like clouds lit by
   the sun.
Let your hair wrap you in softness, in the mists of my delicate
   web.
I am being.

I am what becomes.
I am what is in your womb and in your meeting.
I am the sister in your dance.
I am the dance and the whirling of your silken scarves in the
   wind.
I am the movement.
I am laughter and I am song.
I am the truth of your coming together.
I am the dream you dream.
I am what is not yet born and I am what is forever.

I am the ground and I am the drumming your feet make as they
   stamp the rhythm of creation.
I am the round drum.
I am the heartbeat, faster, more complex, syncopated.
I am the simple beat of your life.

I am the life.
It is so clear, the truth.
It is so complete.

I am the clasp of hands, the open door, the circle around you.
I am wind around the world.
I am the round earth.
I am the dance of stars.
I am the moon dancing.
I am the meeting of the moon, the earth, the sun.
I am the eclipse.
I am everything that moves, that changes, that comes home.

I am the leaping child and I am the womb.
I am the hands that stroke, the body that delights, the breath of
    every kiss.
I am the sister.
I am the Mother.
I am the love set free by your meeting.

You are within and 'round each other, and it is the Mother.
You are one another's breath and it is the Mother.
You join your hands, you join your work, you join your hopes and
    all your bliss and this is the Mother also.
This is what I am.
This is what I am in you and to you and with you always.

Do not be afraid.
I am your dance.
I am your exaltation.
I am your prophecy.

And it shall release the world to God.
And your prophecy will be blest.
And your dance will wind around the world and it will create.
And each of you will give birth to gods.
And the world shall be transformed.
I am the Mother and I tell you this is so.

Mary Speaks

Spirit Father, be beside me on the journey. Heavenly Father be my guide. Be the sureness of my step and the clarity of my direction. Be for me like a pattern of stars that keeps me on my way even at night. Never before have I journeyed alone. Before my father Joachim died he carried me on his back. He knew every path through these hills and beyond, in the desert, and even towards the sea they call Dead. He taught me to find my way by stars, by the drifting of sand, by the smoothness of rocks, and the leaning of trees. He showed me the secret places water is stored, and the way our people glean wild grains and make bread-cakes at mid-day on the hot rocks. He taught me trust. "The heavenly one," he said, "who cares for the songbird and the flower, will surely care for us. We must never be afraid." Heavenly Spirit Father, I am not afraid. Lead me to Elizabeth.

Kinswoman, your face is mine turned old. My greeting echoes in the sound of your voice greeting me. We are made of the same earth. We are one blood. The secrets we bear are cosmic. Yours are fire and water; mine are earth and sky. How could we not love one another? When your house seemed but a bright etching on the umber hills, I sat beneath a fig tree to refresh myself with water and with the ripe fruit. The earth made a lap into which I fit perfectly. You were so close you were already singing in my heart, a melody for the Word singing in my womb. All of us are wrapped 'round one another. Woman bears and is borne by God. My arms are around you; you receive me into your house; no matter where I go forever, we will never be apart.

I dreamed an angel on a Galilean afternoon who whispered your name with the sound of wind through the sycamore trees. Now I look into your eyes and know you. When I saw you first and last I was but a girl of five kissed farewell at the women's court of the temple. All our kin were there. You held my hand and smiled. "Little Mary," you comforted, "we are more than cousins, more than sisters; we are Hokmah and Shekhinah, two faces of the Mother." Because of those words I am not surprised today that you feel in your heart the child I bear in my womb. And more. You tell me who I am. Your recognition brings my womanhood to birth and releases my joy. When I call your name the creation within you quickens with life. Our belief in one another keeps the gift alive.

It beats in us from first breath. Woman is the promise. Woman begins and lives the beginning always. I walked the roads through the hills from Galilee but I gazed down roads of years. I saw faces of women bruised, hardened, emptied of hope. I saw women's bodies drained of life. I saw a great crowd of silent women walking the roads of a devastated world and I called to them but they were wounded. They could not hear my call. I reached my hands to them, pleading, but they were afraid. They had endured too much violence. They did not want to be touched. I sat on a rock by the roadside while they passed me by. I put my head between my knees and wept. I understood the vision. If the women of the world lose faith in themselves, the cycle of beginnings will end. The earth will die. The world will be lost. Only Elizabeth's greeting relieved my grief. "Blessed are you," she cried, "who have believed in the promise. . . ." If one woman only can believe, I say to myself, new worlds can be born.

I sing. The words my sister speaks unlock a wonder in my soul releasing truth in song, in the harmony of holy joy. I become the flute of wisdom, the Sophia of God. I sing the song of the mothers. I hear Hannah in me singing her conception of Samuel the high priest. I sing her song as my own. I sing the song of all the mothers as my own. I sing for all mothers in the futures of all the worlds. And as I sing I become the Mother, Mary, Mara, Mari, Maya, Maat, Ma Nu, Al-Mah, Ma. I become more than who I am, all that I am. I am the Becoming. I am the Mamata, the common blood. I am Ma Nu, the truth. I am Qis-Ma, fate. I am Mah, mother of messiahs. I am immortality. I am the deep. I am the fluid waters—blood, birthing water and milk. My name is the first breath, the first cry, the original song.

My song becomes my dance. Slowly at first then faster, faster. I circle the courtyard of my sister, Elizabeth-house-of-God. My veils billow, whirling round my body. I kick off my sandals; I dance in my bare feet. I wear my skirt on my hips. I roll my belly. I exalt my pregnant belly. I let my belly dance. I let my breasts dance. I dance the dance of becoming, the dance of creative power. My heart beats fast. I stamp my feet. I move to my heart-beat. I move to the beat of the earth. I dance to the mother-beat. Elizabeth enters the ecstasy. Her belly is the full moon. We dance together. We exult the motherlife. We lift our heads and the sound we make is ancient. It is the sound of oceans. It is the sound of earthquakes. It is the sound of the Mother.

The holy is El Shaddai, the breasted one, the womb, compassion. The holy is opening my heart. The holy is pregnant in me with the poor and is offering my breasts to the hungry. The holy makes my lap wide. The holy invites the weeping of all the world to find comfort here. The holy turns my singing into a lullaby for calming fearful hearts, for soothing anxious minds, for reaching the child hidden in everyone. The holy in me rocks the weeping child. The holy smooths my hands into tenderness and with tenderness I bend to touch the lowly. I raise the lowly from their knees. I lift up the lowly from the earth. The Holy One opens my heart. I am wider than the world. I contain the world in gentleness. Everything is alive. Everything is honored. Everything is loved. Love gestures with gentleness. Gentle towards the land, the soil, the rock. Gentle towards everything that grows. Gentle towards the leaf, the grain, the flower, the tree. Gentle towards everything that moves. Gentle towards the bee, the snake, the lamb, the bird. Gentle towards the waters and the air. Gentle towards all peoples. Gentle towards differences. Gentle towards self. Gentleness magnifies our God.

Elizabeth and I dance into stillness. I reach my hand to her belly and touch the leaping child; she rests her fingertips upon the pulse of God. "How shall I deserve that the Mother of my God should come to me?" she whispers and her eyes fill with tears. Both of us are brimming with power and with joy. Both of us believe there is no power greater than this life that connects us. This power makes us equal. This power makes us one.

Together we enter the house of Elizabeth. I am hungry from the journey. I am thirsty from the dance. She spreads a purple cloth and on it places fresh baked bread, wine, and wild red roses in a blue glass vase from Phoenicia. We break the bread and eat. The food is good. She asks of Anna's widowhood. I inquire after Zechariah's voice. She tells the story of the temple angel. I wonder whether Joseph will accept my child. She holds me in her arms and hums a child's song. We don't need much to be filled.

When Elizabeth's child is born the whole town joins the dance. Zechariah sings. Our joy is a flowing well of the purest water. Everyone can drink and be satisfied. It is the longest day of the year. Light lingers over the hills and night will be brief. All night we will dance beneath a million stars and when the morning star rises just before the sun Elizabeth and I will take the child to the hilltop and lift him to the rising dawn.

    Joy in the dance of stars. Joy in the ripe summer wheat. Joy in the full womb. Joy in the birth of worlds. Joy in the circle of holiness out of whom we come forever and ever, world without end. Amen.

THE MERCY OF BIRTH

THE THIRD JOYFUL MYSTERY
THE BIRTH

The Woman Speaks

Mother of mysteries, you filled me with desire, made me pregnant with love. You opened my heart to the waiting, the summons from the land of my former life, the long journey, the star, the birth. We all bear a world child, a child made of stars.

Each of us is birth mother. Each is milk mother. We bear when we can. We birth what is given us to bear. We nourish according to our means. We who are mothers are also children of others. No one is self sufficient.

We are chosen by the child. We mother as the child needs. We give and in the giving discover who we have become. Most of us cannot count them, the children of our bodies, the children of our breasts, the children of our minds, the children of our hearts and souls. They are in our homes, in our neighborhoods, across oceans, in mansions and ghettos. They are laughing and crying and hungry and lost and frightened and curious, and full of the future. They are the world.

Mother of mysteries, I surrender to this pregnancy and birth.

Mother Wisdom Speaks

The round world cries, it leaps, it comes forth.
I am the Mother.
I am the fire that molds the body of promise.
I am the expanding heart.
I am the ocean, from me all life comes.
I am the sky.

Do not forget this.
When you are round with life,
When you feel the kick of becoming deep within you,
When you feel the ripping of your body, your being,
When you know the time has come to bring forth new life,
I am the body.
Ma.
The Mother.

Words cannot contain what I am.
The cry of the child seeks for me.
I am food.
Milk.
Milk pours down over the world,
Milk covers the world, runs down the mountains and becomes
    the sea.
This is the milk of peace, of calm, the milk that nourishes.

I laugh.
I sing a lullaby.
I smooth the tangled nerves of those at war with themselves.
All war begins inside of you.

It is your own child you kill when war erupts.
Be calm.
Accept my peace.
The milk of my breast.
All you need to do is cry out to me.
I am the Mother.

I open myself and you come forth.
I am who you are at every opening of your soul, of your body.
I am who is at every birth.
Every child recognizes me.

I give my blood.
You are born covered in my blood.
The blood of becoming.
The red of passion and energy.
The milk of sacrifice.
When I was the Christ I gave my blood.
And I give blood every day of your lives in the birthing chair.
I crouch over the world and all life comes forth from me.

The sky rains blood.
Ruby.
Crimson light.
It covers everything.
My blood is a dawn of wine.
Drink of me.
Blood is my robe.
I wrap it around you.
It is my love.
It is what I give.

I drain myself into you and over you.
I cover you with my life.
I am the Mother.

Mary Speaks

Abba of the rocky way, Abba of desert nights, Abba of mountain passages, protect us. Joseph walks beside me and places his large, gentle hand on the small of my back where the pain, in these last days of pregnancy, thickens its throbbing. The pain is a long pulling against my spine. At night I cannot sleep and during the day I keep silence. Joseph sings. Joseph's song is a space wide enough to walk through. Joseph's song is a room where I can rest and await birth despite the constant turbulence of the journey. Joseph is my Abba of the way. When, in my heart, I cry out to you, oh holy God, Joseph turns and smiles. He offers me water. Holy Father of the mountains and the stars, your wisdom planted the seed, but Joseph is the father of my child.

When the census order came I cried. It is the birth time, I said to Joseph, I cannot make a journey, I cannot go to Bethlehem. We could die. While all the time I knew. I saw. Bethlehem the small, Bethlehem of the golden grain, Bethlehem where the poor have bread, Bethlehem whose shepherds Yahweh anoints as kings, David's Bethlehem, city of Adonai—door into being, gateway of life, threshold God, vulva God, birthing God. Adonai's Bethlehem. There is no better place for birth. Even Caesar is the servant of God.

°O°○°O°

The innkeeper's face is flint. He looks at me from the sides of his eyes. He shakes his head. Inside the walls camels grunt and raucous men encourage the dancing girls. No laboring mothers allowed. It would not be right. He turns us away and the heavy doors to the enclosure slowly swing shut. My body quakes. Joseph turns the donkey towards the hills.

°O°○°O°

Earth, hold me on your sturdy lap for I am your daughter and my birthing is your own. Earth, receive me into your deep cave and encircle me there while the child struggles forth from my own body's cave. Earth, cool me when my body fires. Earth, absorb the water from my womb, seawater, passover water, tears. Earth, be anointed with the blood of birth. Earth, be my birthing chair. Earth, echo all my screams. Earth, tremble with my ecstasy. Earth, mother of all, upon your bed of loam, within your shelter of rock, let me bring forth our child.

°O°○°O°

At home in Nazareth a large grey cat chose the corner of my kitchen for her kittening. For a month she carried bits of fluff that gathered 'round my loom—strings, tiny bits of cloth, soft grasses from the yard, some shavings from Joseph's wood shop—all to make herself a bed. She worked and then she tried it out, circling, forming a nest, resting, licking her dainty paws. She became my teacher. I think she knew I needed her. Here, in this cave, a large ox shelters. I lean against her where she lies; I share her warmth; she calms me with the steady beating of her heart. Joseph gathers grasses for my birthing bed. A sparrow feeds her young.

Oh Adonai, threshold of life, birthgate; Oh Elah, mother of all; Elohim, who breaks the inner waters, El Shaddai, breast-God, milk-giver; Shekhinah, in-dweller God of my woman's heart, woman's womb,[5] assist me now! This is not as I had planned. Where is the midwife? Birth takes my body; I am not mine, I am the child's. Oh Holy One, who breathed the world into being, breathe in me. I am earth quaking. I am torn. Earth groans. Earth gasps. Earth is rent, she screams. I am no one. I am every woman. I am earth. I am at the mercy of birth.

Suddenly silence. Waves of wonder. Self absorbed in totality. No pain but an ecstasy of being. No time; an eternity between breaths. The release of life. I float upward from silken dark. I see Joseph's face and his eyes are stars. I hear a tiny cry. God. In every birth, God.

I am milk. I flow white. I am the nourisher of worlds; of one small child. The child's mouth sucks, my body becomes food. The child's hands hold the cup of my breast; the child's eyes absorb my soul. I withhold nothing that the child needs.

An old woman silhouetted against the full moon stands at the mouth of the cave. "We heard a crooning in the stars," she tells Joseph, "and we came to see what kind of birth could turn the night into a lullaby." She kneels beside the child and me. Her body smells of musk and her breath is yeasty with new wine. The men hover at a distance. Birth awes them. "Your child called us to your side," she whispers in my ear. She slips her spidery hands under the child's head and gently lifts him to the view of her family and her friends. I let him go. Moonlight bathes his face. "This night Elohim has given us a child," she cries and the tattered crowd kneels. "Behold," she prophecies to the infant that she holds, "your people welcome you."

I thought I dreamed the singing. Heaven and earth turned, opened and released a bliss beyond imagining. Light waved across the sky like the path of wings. Stars fell by the thousands. I held my breath, and released it slowly like a sigh. The universe was singing. I saw the end of tears, the end of death, the end of unjust pain; and the end was a beginning of peace, a world of compassion, a cry of glory. Heaven and earth opened and gave birth to bliss. The singing crescendos; this is not a dream, this is in my heart; this opens my soul infinitely. I am the earth. I am the sky. And my child—my child is bliss. My child is the future of the world.

The sky is silent now. The shepherds returned to the fold. Jesus and Joseph sleep. Now in the common night I am simply Mary, mother of a child. Was the song but wind in the myrtle trees? Is every woman's child divine? His soft black hair curls on the light bronze of his forehead. His breathing is a miracle. If from now until the fullness of life, he lives only as my common little boy I promise I will not forget. When my child was born the world's poor ones heard the angel's song.

Glory where the stars whirl and light a midnight sky. Glory for a world never ending but beginning over and over in births of every kind—womb children, dream children, heart children. Glory to the child, opener of doors. Glory to the child, promising tomorrow. Glory to the child who is every child and one child, now and forever, world without end.

A Letting Go Like Rain

The Fourth Joyful Mystery

The Presentation of Jesus and

Purification of Mary

The Woman Speaks

Mother of mysteries, on a morning in mid-September it began to rain. First the thunder awakened me, then the downpour. I welcomed it. Gusts. Mists. Steady soaking of a sun-cracked ground. Brilliant California summer had begun to taste dusty, and I longed for the fresher climate of my Minnesota childhood.

The wet concrete of the patio felt cool on my bare feet when I went outside to lift my face to the rain. The fevered earth let go to the soothing coolness. Crisp hills hardened by the constant sun yielded to a softening grace. In their dark burial place the shrivelled seeds thrilled to the touch of water and opened with the ecstasy of new life. In a world where letting go is the natural process of life, why is it so difficult for me?

I have never let go easily. I hold tenaciously to what I am and love despite what I've been taught again and again of transformation. My heart clenches around my life and resists the relentless unfolding of creation until I am forced open by some explosion of change. When the shock passes I breathe more easily until I tighten up again. I am California without rain. These California hills harden and crack in the relentless sun. Wild flowers die in a ground that, barren, yearns for the blessing of rain. The sky will not let go. The sky resists even the clouds.

All that I am, all that I have, all to which I've given birth I must let go. Help me, Mother, because for me it is a release as difficult as California summer rain.

Mother Wisdom Speaks

I am gentle.
I am the rain, the letting go.
I am what you surrender and in surrendering you become what
   you let go.
I am your life, your green becoming.
I am the flower and the grass.
I am the rain.
I wash you.
I make your face shine.
I wash away your fear, your hardening.
I am the ground wherein your seed of life waits.
I am the rain.
Release me.

I will cover you.
I will moisten you.
I will make you soft.
Be pliable in me.
It is not difficult.
Don't work at it.
Let go.
Love.
Turn your face to me with love.
Love the hardness itself and you will soften it.

Love the barren earth and you will turn it into a garden.
I am the love that you let go.

Release me into the dry world.
Release me into your thirsty heart.
I am the rain.

Take off your clothes, your protection, your fear, and lie naked on
   the hopeful ground.
Extend your arms.
Open your eyes.
Implore the sky.
This is your surrender.
This is your faith.
Have no control.
Open your hand.
Release the tight fist your fingers make.
Let go.

I will rain on you.
I will turn you to water.
I will make of your mind and of your heart a fertile plain.
You will never be thirsty again.

You are a cup.
You are a round, empty cup.
I will fill you.
I will pass you around to the people.
I will never let you be empty again.
You will feel the water in you like an ocean.

Boundless.
The water of life will rise up.
No one around you will be dry.
Only let go.

You think you can hold on to me.
You think that if you close your fist,
That if you squeeze your eyes shut,
If you make your heart tight,
Then love cannot escape.
I am love and I cannot be controlled.
I am the Mother.
I am what is given.

Let go.
You will find me.
I will rain on you.
I will fill you and you will be endless.

Mary Speaks

This road from Bethlehem to the temple in Jerusalem is rough;
dust disturbed by our steps lifts on the wind. Dust is on my
tongue and darkens the face of my child. On a day when rain had
settled the earth and flowers blanketed the land I could have
danced my offering; I could have lifted our child over my head
and sung the ancient song my mother sang, and all the women
sing. I would have sung while Jesus laughed and Joseph freed the
doves into the brilliant sky. Father, open my heart and free my
feet to dance upon the dust. Let what I offer be the rain.

°O°O°O°

From this distance the temple seems a pearl adorning the breast of earth, or perhaps a drop of sweet milk glistening in the morning sun. My own breasts thrill and come alive to Jesus's nuzzling. He sucks and I am satisfied. Now that I see the temple on the hill I go to her like going to my larger self. She is the image of earth containing God. She is the Mother. When we enter her gates we approach the womb of God. Our gift impregnates her. She surrounds the law with wisdom and whoever goes to her finds what they seek. She gives birth to whatever we offer.

°O°O°O°

The old man, Simeon, stands at the gate watching as he stood watching when I was a girl and was brought here to the women's court to learn the mysteries from the women we called wise. I remember that he smiled on me but looked beyond my eyes. He was like a gnarled tree rooted at the world's edge. We named him Sentinel. Today Simeon's eyes stop and rest on the infant I carry. There is no need to look beyond. He reaches out and waits without a word. Worlds meet and touch; the old man holds my child.

°O°O°O°

We wonder at the old man's words not because we have not known, but because he also knows the song the angels sang. He speaks and something flutters in my womb as though the child he lifts to the morning sun lives within me still. The child is my yearning towards tomorrow. The sentinel speaks true. We walk in the light that floods from our wombs' rich darkness.

When Simeon returns the child and lifts his hands I know that he will die. His eyes have the look of those who pour out their lives. The promise of the Holy One is born; the waiting time has passed. The law is a gnarled tree on the world's edge outlined against the rising dawn. Simeon's hands tremble with God. We are wrapped in blessing like air filled with lightning.

I will live forever in the old man's dying words. When he spoke I saw myself standing on the threshold between worlds, connecting them, but being torn in the deep core of my living heart. I felt a dying that could take two thousand years or more. I stood on the threshold holding my child like a seal upon my heart and felt the jeers and hatred of those who resist the coming of God. I stood beneath the gnarled tree at the edge of the world and suddenly my child was fastened there and I threw my arms around the rough wood and I could not move and my child could not move. It was our destiny.

I hear drumming. The old man speaks but I can't hear his words; I hear the heartbeat of the world. You wonder if I hear the deep sound in the soul of the mother whose child is marked at birth with a scarlet splash across her face. I hear. The mother whose child is blind, or lame, or cannot speak. I hear. The mother whose child dreams worlds his peers won't share. I hear. The mother whose child must live where it is wrong to live. I hear. The mother whose child weeps while all the others laugh and talks to birds and tries to heal the sparrow that the others tried to kill. I hear. These children are my child. The drumming in my heart is for them all.

I have always been afraid of swords. They divide. They separate the body from the soul, breath from the beating heart. They drain the people's blood. When soldiers came from Rome to Nazareth brandishing their swords my people bent to the dust and said "yes" to anything. His sword gave Caius power to rape young Lydia while the women hid and our townsmen hung their heads. Oh, I know our father, David, pierced the enemies of our people with the sword; as Solomon did, as did the Maccabees, as did Moses in the ancient times, and Joshua who bears my child's name, and our sister Judith of the valiant heart. But my soul! These divisions, they pierce my soul!

What are these thoughts that tumble from the schism in a mother's heart? Can I endure such motherhood? What secrets can be worthy? I want to know. The old man's prophecy has opened up in me a sacred place of power secreted away since Sarah's time and since the day that Rachel stole the Hearth-Goddess from her father's house and brought her to the tent of Israel. Is the secret Rachel hid beneath her skirts the very secret hidden in women's hearts for centuries?

°O°O°O°

Anna takes me in her arms. She is warm and smells like fresh bread. "Mary, little Mary," she croons while Joseph smiles and old Simeon rests from his seizure of prophecy. "And the baby, ah. Look at him, our little love, our son." Anna does not rant and rave of kings and saviors; she is a woman; she looks at me. I know what she sees. "I felt you were the favored one," she whispers so the menfolk do not hear, "I felt it since I held you on my lap and told you tales of she who mothers all. I felt it when you danced the dance of veils at your betrothal. Now I see her mercy in your eyes and her compassion in the breasts that feed this child. Ah, he is beautiful. And we know who he is, my little Mary; we know who he is." Old Anna kisses me. Both our hearts are opened. The secrets are beginning to be told.

Now I can let him go. Despite the vision of the gnarled tree, I can let him go. Despite the swords. No splitting of my soul can stop me. Not pain, not loss, not death itself can quench this joy of what we are and the wonder our surrender will release. I can let him go and dance while the Levite lifts my child from the earth, above the altar to the stars. It is our destiny. I can let him go.

°O°O°O°

Glory to the one yearning for release from the secret places of the heart, from the hiding place of earth, from the tangles of mind, from the careful unconsciousness of soul, from the caves, from the night, from the turning moon, from the womb. Glory be.

BLUE BEADS LOST IN DESERT SAND

THE FIFTH JOYFUL MYSTERY

THE FINDING OF JESUS IN THE TEMPLE

The Woman Speaks

Mother of mysteries, we women, we have deserts in our hearts. We wander there. We all have lost. Someone. Something. We've lost sons. We've lost daughters. We've lost dreams and the innocence of our childhood hopes. We have lost things small and large. A favorite dish; a home. We've lost our truth, sometimes, protecting someone else's name. We've lost ourselves in the cloak of someone else's power.

We light candles. We wander at night. We seek to find what we lost. Our eyes become hawklike, looking.

Mother Wisdom Speaks

Nothing is lost.
All is within you.
Rise from your knees.
Rise and see.

There is nothing I have not hidden in my eyes.
Look at me.

The light you seek is there.
The love is there.
The life you thought you lost, you only let it go a moment.
It is in my eyes.

Come into my eyes.
Let go.
Release yourself.
I love you.
See my love.
Everything you love, everything that you hold dear,
All you base your life upon—here it is.
I hold it for you, safe, in my eyes.
I love you.

Look at me.
Look into me.
I let you in.
The barriers you feel, you have built them,
Block by block and stone upon each stone.
You have made them thick and tight with the mortar of your
    fears.
Fear not.
I hold everything that you desire.
I am the home for all you believe to be lost.
Nothing is lost.
Everything comes home to me.
I am the Mother.

Feel my gentleness.
Feel my love.

Oh, my heart expands with tenderness for you.
My smile beacons through the night.
No night is dark when you are coming home to me.

Nothing is truly lost.
I keep your child.
I keep the sons and daughters of your pain,
I keep the children of your joy.
You need not be afraid.
They are safe as you are safe.
I hold them all.
Nothing is lost.
Nothing is lost.
Nothing is ever lost.

You are my darling one.
You are my beloved.
See me.
Look into my eyes.
Come in through my open eyes.
Everything you thought you lost is there.
I hold it.
I am its home.
I am the Mother.

Take my hand.
I reach out for you.
It is not really dark.
Your love, it is not really lost.
I hold you.

Feel my hand.
You are already in my arms.
You are already looking at me.
Open your eyes.
Open your eyes, my dear one.
You are my dearest child.
I am your Mother.
Do not be afraid.
Nothing is lost.
Nothing that you love is lost.
I am its home.
I am where everything is full, where all of life is complete.
The darkness is the pathway through my eyes.
You will find light.
You will begin to see.

Call on me.
Reach out your hand.
I love you.
You are my darling child.
You are my dearest heart.
Do not be afraid.
Nothing is lost.
Nothing.
Everything is right here, right here in me.
I am your Mother.

Mary Speaks

Our boy is gone. I looked in every tent, asked every child, pleaded with our kin. Old Phanuel was bedding down the beasts and told me not to fret; Jesus is a boy, he laughed, and boys will do what boys will do. I wept, hiding behind my veil. He could be dead. What about the bandits of the hills? He could be captured, enslaved, like Joseph of the tale we tell on winter nights circled round the fire. He would not have run away. Not my child.

I have lost a lot of things. The first veil made by my mother's mother when she was but a girl. It was rough spun stuff and woven crooked just a bit. I left it in the sycamore outside the village where I played when I was young. My mother wept and sent me after it but it was gone. A string of lapis beads from Joseph when we were betrothed. I wore them like a promise everywhere and always. It was in Egypt they were lost, somewhere along the road where we spent a night without a moon. I've lost much simpler things: my favorite needle made of bone, the clasp that Joseph carved to hold my cloak in place when it is cold and I am drawing water from the well, a pale blue cup, a clear carnelian stone. Tonight my hands hunger to touch these things. I would lay my head on the rough weave of my grandmother's veil and again and again, through my tears, whisper the name of my child.

Tonight we can do nothing. We listen to the wind. We wait. Joseph paces past the fire. While I watch he stops; he turns his gaze to the invisible hills and his body bends against the fire's light like that of some abandoned God whose image stands broken where once the young men danced. He looks to be the ruin of a man. After this night he will never not be old.

I will not sleep. The nightbird calls; a desert lion prowls the outer circle of the camp. The watchman listens for a child's cry but not as I listen. I have schooled my heart to Jesus's every breath so that for thirteen years I have rested only in his breathing. His dreams awaken me so I am kneeling by his mat the moment that he starts from sleep and calls my name. How can he be lost? I would have felt him go. Such absence would have split my soul. I cannot sleep tonight; I will sit facing East listening for the breathing of my child. Wherever he may be I will surround him like a lullaby and he will sleep in peace.

When I lost the lapis beads we retraced our steps to where I last remembered wearing them. Each round pebble seemed a clue. Beads scatter from a broken cord. I searched in clumps of grass and broke my fingernails digging in the sand one place I thought I saw a glint of blue. We walked, zig-zagging back along the road, our eyes sweeping every inch of ground. If I could have found just one blue bead I would have treasured it like the midnight sky for all my life. As the sickle of the moon fell beneath the twilight we returned where we began. Joseph looked at me as if to say, "The beads are gone but you will wear my promise always as earth wears the lapis sky."

°O°O°O°

At dawn our kin spiraled outward from the camp calling Jesus's name. Rebecca thought she heard him whimper from behind some rocks. She cried, "He's here!" and we followed her, scrambling up a stone outcropping toward the sound. It was but a lamb caught in a bramble. Young Asher saw a speck of red appear and disappear across the plains and thought it must be Jesus's coat. We found just a tattered blanket blown here and there by desert winds. I lost him more than twenty times today. Whenever I close my eyes tonight to rest from hope and fear I see him in Jerusalem.

°O°O°O°

Jerusalem's towers and sprawling streets lie just below. It is the third day. I want to run to the temple. I want to cry his name. I know that he is here. He would be sheltered by the temple like a womb. But my heart is tight with unwept tears. If he is in the temple could God have wished it so? When Sarah lost her only son because his father heard the voice of God, she also must have wondered and wept. How she must have run across the burning sand to meet him when he stumbled down the mountain with old Abraham blinded by fire. That night she must have arisen from her sleep a hundred times to look at Isaac and she must have asked the darkness, "Why are mothers not consulted in these things?"

°O°O°O°

I saw him first as any mother might, simply safe. He looked at us and smiled as if we'd never been apart. "We've sought you, sorrowing," said Joseph and his voice was weighted with the desert nights and millennia of desert sand. I saw my son. I had not seen him quite this way before. "Why did you seek me?" His inquiry was innocent and wise. He had expected us to know. I saw our future in him then, the truth of all our lives. We all live in one another's love. No one can be lost. I turned within, listened to the voice of my heart and he was there as he had always been.

He came with us. I had looked into the eyes of my son and seen God. Now he came along like any other little boy.

All that was years ago. Our son returned to Nazareth to learn wisdom from simple things of earth. Joseph taught him how to work with wood, respect the natural grain, rub it with the wax of bees until it glowed. With our cousin, Nathaniel, Jesus learned the art of growing grain to yield a hundredfold of fruit. He reaped at harvest-time and brought home riches from the earth from which we made delicious bread. He carried the basket for me when we observed the Feast of Loaves, sharing our riches of food with those more needy than ourselves: Saul, the crippled boy, and Rachel, who was blind. We go to synagogue and he learns the wisdom of the law. He also listens to the birds and asks me, "Where is the beginning of the wind?"

°O°O°O°

His eyes are lapis, deeper than the night and clear. All my life when silence wraps me like a shawl I will close my eyes and wonder at these things. I will gather bright blue beads wherever they are scattered in my heart and join them on a cord. What I have sought is in my heart. I wear it like a promise.

Glory in the Mother's heart. Glory where our life begins and to the home from which we walk to seek our names. Glory that our lives are scattered beads around the world. Glory to the one in whom nothing is lost.

Mysteries of Sorrow

Transform me

Bring me through fear, pain and death

Into the fullness of love

Yesterday mists hung on tree branches like tears on lashes so that looking through them I saw rainbows. A month of days and nights has passed since the earthquake and still each creaking of the house triggers my adrenaline. I've considered moving out of California, so have some friends. Martha says she still might go. She cries at night. Her marriage broke apart a year ago but it took the quake to start the tears. Jan, my neighbor down the street whose husband died last Fall, huddles wrapped around her three-year-old son whenever there's an aftershock. She says she doesn't sleep. "No matter what you say to explain it," writes Suzanne from Minnesota, "I don't believe that I can imagine the earth moving. My immediate reaction is terror at the thought; what would I do with the experience?"

While I stared at the mist thinking how lovely, how various, how many-mooded nature is, Kathy called. Her father-in-law had died. Cancer prolonged the passage but the death was sudden as it always is. A surprise. "You can't believe he isn't breathing anymore. There is a time he is alive and before the hand on the clock can move he's dead and there is nothing you can do ever again. Something splits apart, there is a shiver and it's done. You think you can depend on life. You can't."

I thought, how like the earth we are.

Earth shifts and splits and sorrow is released. It seeps from the wound like blood, slow and warm. It sticks to you and dries there. You keep looking at the place that broke and changed forever and you know there is nothing you can do to make it like it was before. Sometimes a side of mountain breaks away and falls into the sea. You can't believe it. You stare at the gap in the earth; there's sky there. It should be beautiful. Years from now people will come who never saw it as it was and they will say it's beautiful. They will marvel at the granite precipice from which the rock sheered and dropped. They will pitch their tents on the beach and paint the giant rock against which waves crash and thunder. They will try to match sheerness with sheerness in their minds, imagining the mountain as it was, but they will fail. They won't be sad. They'll say they're sure they like it better now. The breaking brought the beauty out in ways no one could see before.

Sorrow pours out of us when what we loved is gone and cannot be brought back because it is changed completely. Sorrow is an energy pouring out through what is split in us. It is what is left of what connected us and made us whole. It is blood seeping out. It is what remains of life-as-it-was before a quake surprised us and left us being someone we can't recognize.

These are the mysteries of sorrow. The face of the Mother, scarred and shadowed, is the face of Anath—the aged Goddess, feared, cut off, abandoned in the deep places of dreams we name nightmares. This is the face we reject; we call it anathema; we say that Hers is not any face of the divine but of evil. Yet we call on her. "Maranatha," we cry. She is the end, the precipice, the void, the falling mountain, the splitting of the earth, the bleeding out, the last breath, the step off the world's edge. Anath is death's quake, that sheer gasp of transformation.

She is dark of the moon. She is eclipse. She is the turning. She is the change. When Jesus hung between earth and heaven in the passion that transformed the world, Anath darkened the sun, quaked and split the earth, tore the temple veil, released the dead, hid Eli's face. Anath was death transforming everything. Hers is the face in the mirror reflecting the end of this life, the sorrow of release. Hers is the quake that rolls the stone from the door of the tomb.

Anath's image in us is that of the crone. I figure Mary's age at nearly fifty when her son died. Mary was a menopausal woman, a young crone. According to ancient belief, her creative blood ceased flowing in order to congeal within her into "wise blood;" she would give birth to wisdom.

Women's mysteries, however, have been much ignored. The crone mysteries are the most ignored of all.

Jesus died of domination, of his world's dualistic power structures. The Mother's Anath-face looked on that destructive world with the eyes of death. Jesus cried, "It is finished," and the world began to change. The dying takes centuries and Anath's face strikes horror in those who resist the beauty that will come. Mary, standing where the cross towered at the epicenter of the quake, wears Anath's face. Mary, suddenly old, covered with mud and blood, weighted with her dead son, washing his pale skin with rain, wears Anath's face.

These sorrowful mysteries are hers. They are the mysteries of all women. They mark the passage of the crone. These are the mysteries of death and transformation, of expanding our souls in order to live with loss and dissolve our fear.

Mary mirrored every sorrow of her son. But she had already traversed the passage. In each mystery he must have looked on her to see the other side. The crone endures the agony of fear in confronting the end of her life and is filled with wise blood. Disfigurement, degradation, exhaustion and abandonment accompany her passage into the shadow of Anath. She looks into the mirror of herself until she doesn't flinch at what she sees, and so she is transformed, becomes a moral judge and guide through the passages of life and death. The mysteries of sorrow are hers as well as his.

It's a November afternoon unlike the one two days ago when I began this writing about sorrow. Sun casts a slanted light that intensifies the gold and picks up the new green that's burst out after our California rains. The earth seems so solid and secure. Today I can't believe it moved and imperceptibly is moving now upward toward Alaska. I might take my puppy, Ana, for a walk. There's Jan, my neighbor, on the sidewalk out in front. She is laughing with her son.

WISE BLOOD

THE FIRST SORROWFUL MYSTERY

THE AGONY IN THE GARDEN

The Woman Speaks

Mother of mysteries, I am the age that Mary must have been when Jesus died. I've seen death. I've felt how thin that membrane is that wraps our souls in flesh. I've heard the whisper when it tears. Life is so delicate. So transparent. I could see right through it if I opened wide my eyes. Nothing can be held so well it will be safe.

When menses stops time's circle doesn't close. An unfamiliar waiting, not for birth, begins. The circle is larger than I thought. It is not the circle of the moon now, monthly changing shadow to light. Instead it is the universe, a fireball where shadow and light combine and I can see neither the beginning nor the end for they are the same. I've had the end of safety. I am dying. What is being born?

Mother Wisdom Speaks

You store up blood.
It is no longer red.
Your blood is black and thick; it is the density of life.
It is wise blood.

You make no more sons and daughters.
You make wisdom of your womb.

Go inside.
Exist where beginnings and endings are one.
Stare down your fear.
Look it in the eyes until it falls on its knees.
Eat your fear.
Digest it.
Take it into your blood.
It makes you strong.

Your body is the world.
Everything fears death.
Matter groans, waiting.
You are what is most aware.
You are my body.
You are my beloved one.
Feel the fear.
Turn it to your blood.
Pour it out.
Black.
Thick.
Beautiful.
The blood of an old woman.
The blood of one who no longer fears death,
Of one who stands on the edge of the world and sings.

I sing in you.
I am your black blood.
I am your richness.

I am what is left when fear dissolves.
I am forever.

I won't say, do not be afraid.
Use your fear.
Take up your blood.
Wash your hands in it.
Smear it on rocks.
Make an offering.
You are the priest of the coming age.
Your blood is the passing of death's angel.

Mark your doorposts.
Mark your mountains.
Mark the stones all along the coast.
The dolphins need to see it.
The birds will know you have been there.
Mark the edges of your fields and make the secret sign around
   your cities, on power plants and where they dump their waste.
Your blood is holy.
It is the last blood.
It is the end of an age.
It is the transformation of fear.
Let it flow.
Let it flow.

Empty yourself.
I am what remains.
I am the clear place.
I am the open.
I am the spirit womb when your body's womb has shrivelled and
   is dry.

I am the radiant golden womb of your creations yet to come.
I am your consciousness of life.

Take your walking stick and go out into the world shining.
Wherever you walk the people will find peace.
I will draw lines on your face to make it soft.
I will make my gentleness a pool in your eyes.
I will make your hands strong.
Work.
Let your work flow like breathing.
No work is unworthy.
Do what is needed.
Do what you can.
Do what you enjoy.
You are fashioning a world.

Once you have lost your fear there is nothing left to lose.
Give everything away.

I am the Mother.
I have preceded you.
I have awaited you.
I am within you.
I am where you will go and I am the world you will create.

Mary Speaks

Abba, I have had enough of wandering. But when Jesus asked "Why is this night different. . ." at the Pesch and as the sun sank behind the temple hill, I knew. And when he raised the cup and spoke of blood, I knew. And when he broke the bread. I let him wash my feet and when he dried them with the towel I knew that we would wander yet again. I knew it in the tone of Peter's voice and when Mary shook the tambourine and danced to Miriam's song. When John embraced my son, I knew. I knew when Judas closed the door. Now my son walks through the night and toward the olive grove. Now I know our wandering is towards the world's edge; our purpose, to pass over.

This is the night of blood. This is the night when Miriam and Moses drew the sign of life in blood across our doors against the angel, Death. This is the night our wandering began and ends. This is where we stay; the blood is on our foreheads now; the blood is on our hands. We wade in blood. We are the people of blood. I am not ashamed of this. But I have no blood this year to mark the post above my door. I await the sound of wings.

On Winter Solstice of the year just past I ceased my flow of blood. As I had done so many times before, I found a quiet place and sat alone. A woman of my years could cease her flow at any time. We cannot know for sure. Always I give honor to my days of blood. My first blood I left on moss beneath the giant trees of Lebanon. It was my secret that I could not tell my father, Joachim, or he would have thought himself unclean. I never could believe my blood unclean. My final flow of blood came hard. Five days of blood and then it ceased. It never flowed again. One day I let it flow into a stream where I sat naked underneath the sky.

One day I used it to anoint a dying child. One day I rubbed it on my skin and prayed for the fertility of earth. One day I sat with women in our tent; Jael's first blood flowed and we combined her young blood with my old and offered it to the Mother of us all. On the last day of my blood I went to where the round rock lies beside the sacred cave. I prayed. I marked the rock with blood.

The mothers say my blood is wise. The mothers know. I know the fear I feel tonight walks naked through the streets of Jerusalem. My fear is full of blood but I do not feel wise. My fear is an old woman in a purple cloak that is to the priest but a shadow on the temple wall. My fear sees and my fear hears. I hear the sound of silver tinged with blood that is not women's blood, falling, rolling down the cobbled street away from the temple gate.

Mary sits with me and Salome. We spin by hand the soft wool of the Passover lamb. Twisting, twisting, binding fibers into yarn. None of us can sleep. We whisper dreams we fear will die this night. Mary stops and says she thinks a dream once seen can never be denied; it will be dreamed and dreamed down roads of years until it will be real. I am older and of dreams I know the truth. They can be killed. They are fragile, dreams. A little hardening of soul and they disappear. They are like the rainbow; they need tears and hope. But I do not speak. Perhaps among us we have gentleness enough to nurture any dream. I twist the wool. I dream I spin a world.

When Jesus went from Nazareth to seek his cousin John I was afraid. John was outcast as the prophets often are. Elizabeth journeyed over the hills and when I took her in my arms she wept. What mother ever understands her son? "Why must he be alone?" she cried, "Why so burning and so filled with storm? I feel it will end painfully. Mary, why would God give us sons just to let them die?" I didn't know. It was the fear I lived with every day. So when Jesus took the cloak I weaved without a seam, and when he smiled and kissed my hands and eyes, and when he said his time had come and he must leave our home I wept. I wept for one whole day and then I dried my tears. I went to walk beside my son.

°O°O°O°

Death is not the greatest of my fears. I am afraid of wasted time. I am afraid that what we held so certainly is false. I am afraid I didn't understand. When the Word was spoken in my womb its meaning was a whisper. But for the angel I have no reason to believe this son of mine is more than any other man. And the angel was a sigh of truth, a caress of light more felt than heard or seen. If I cried out tonight for proof would it be granted me? I will not cry. His eyes are proof enough; his hands, the way they touch the poor of body and of soul. I will wait here on the edge of time and I will hold my fear in a cup of clay and I will gaze on it. For I believe that even if he dies for what he's done I will go on living in his dream. I will drink from the cup of clay until my fear is gone. And I, I will go on.

We were made wild with love. Earth opened up her heart and we saw splendor there—in children's eyes, in a handful of grain given in a field by a stranger who had more than needed for the evening's bread, in nights so silent sleeping under stars, in the laughter of the poor. The world is radiant with God. We became so wild we walked the narrow valleys danger stalked. We believed the enemy could be a friend. We danced with those who would. We shared our wine and bread and bound the wound of a Samaritan who had fallen in with thieves. They warned us this could end in death, those who walked the wider road of law.

I will go to stand, now, underneath the moon. She has risen since he left the upper room to find his silence and his name. He went to find the will of God, he said. What is this will? It cannot be his death, although that death could be the splash of red upon a weave of blues that startles us with truth. It is our need to see that prompts such startling and not the will of God. I know the will of God. It is the spinning of the thread. It is the fabric, whole and without seams, and all the colors balanced, beautiful. And when the cloth is whole, it is the cutting from the loom.

°O°O°O°

Jesus spoke of death as though he could not die. It is not his death He fears. I remember when he was a boy, he brought a rabbit in to me. The little creature's leg was torn from a trap. Jesus tried to set the leg but when he touched the wound the rabbit screamed and died. My child cried. I sought to comfort him; "It was merciful she died," I said. "No, mother. It is not the death; it is the trap—it is the scream that makes me cry." Tonight it is the torn world he could not heal that brings his tears. The trap has shut. We all are fastened there.

Now I hear the shouts. Now I see the torches flame. Now is the height, now is the end of fears. God can do nothing when the world goes mad. Now is the death of dreams. The threads are cut with swords. Peter runs to me. His scabbard's empty and his eyes are filled with tears.

Glory at the world's edge. Glory where the sky rains blood. Glory for the will to let ourselves be wise. Glory in the aged womb, in the fragile dream, in the severed thread, in the sacrifice for love. Glory for those who hope, who drink from the cup of fear, who take the hand of the Angel of Death. Glory for the hands that hold a screaming world.

A Dream of Bones

The Second Sorrowful Mystery

The Scourging at the Pillar

.

The Woman Speaks

Mother of mysteries, the woman of earth walks, head high, strength in her bones, a jewel in her head, beauty in her stride. She walks everywhere in the world. She leaps over barriers that are crumbling. She enters rooms where decisions are made and she makes her wisdom known. She speaks for all that cannot speak because their voices have been robbed. She stands as mother to all that has been stripped and torn apart, all that has been scattered and seems irretrievable. Her voice roars like the ocean and she will be heard. She stands for the violently stripped—the rainforests, the mountains, the farmland, whole species of animals near extinction: elephants for ivory, gorillas for their hands, wolves for their ability to mirror our fears. She stands for each of us: minds stripped of creative thought, souls stripped of confidence, hearts stripped of enthusiasm. She is our shaman now. She wears your body. Your love glows in her eyes. We see the shining of her jewel. She is your daughter, your promise that we will be whole.

Mother Wisdom Speaks

Some of you I will hollow out.
I will make you a cave.
I will carve you so deep the stars will shine in your darkness.
You will be a bowl.
You will be the cup in the rock collecting rain.

I will hollow you with knives.
I will not do this to make you clean.
I will not do this to make you pure.
You are clean already.
You are pure already.

I will do this because the world needs the hollowness of you.
I will do this for the space that you will be.
I will do this because you must be large.
A passage.
People will find their way through you.
A bowl.
People will eat from you and their hunger will not weaken them
    unto death.
A cup
To catch the sacred rain.

My daughter, do not cry.
Do not be afraid.
Nothing you need will be lost.
I am shaping you.
I am making you ready.

I will hollow out your bones.
They will be light as the bones of birds.
You will fly.
You will soar over the oceans.
You will see what needs to be done.
The wind will pass through you as though you were a flute, a
    shepherd's pipe.
Your music will soothe troubled minds and turn fear into a mist
    that dissolves at morning.

I will hollow the center of you.
I will open up your womb.
I will expand you.
You will bear worlds.
You will give birth to ideas.
You will be the round room of compassion and souls will wait in
    you, resting, knowing they can be reborn.
Your children will not be one or twelve, they will be multitudes.
You will not be able to count them.
Your life will become a womb.
Your soul, a creator, through this hollowing.
I will carve you out and your blood will be a river.
Your blood will become one with the sea's blood.
Your blood will rise with the tides.
It will cry out to the moon.
And there will be no end to its crying.
It will flow with the blood of all the world,
    the blood of war,
    the blood of children wounded,
    birthing blood,
    blood shed on rocks,

blood nourishing the earth.
It will flow together, it will swell and it will cry out to the moon.

Light will flow in your hollowing.
You will be filled with light.
Your bones will shine.
The round, open center of you will be radiant.
I will call you Brilliant One.
I will call you Daughter Who Is Wide.
I will call you Transformed.

Mary Speaks

Abba, what did the high priest see when he removed the temple veil? Did he see you as I did when my father took me to the trees in Lebanon? Did he hear you sing? Were all the secrets in his heart revealed? Did he laugh and cry and want to dance and throw himself to earth before you and feel his tears moistening the rich and fertile soil? Did he smell the good musk of his createdness?

He must not have seen. He would have recognized your son.

I went to the courtyard of Roman law. I saw the thing that used to be my son. I stood where they say it is unclean to stand. Why should "unclean" bother me? Until my days of wise blood I was unclean each month; I was, myself, a courtyard forbidden. I stood and saw the violence the laws of man can do when they have killed the spirit of the heart. I heard the shouts of those with empty souls. They want to kill my son. They are afraid and angered by their fear. They think their world will end and they will not give up their power over all our lives. And so they want to kill my son who says that God speaks equally to children as to priests and kings.

The soldiers scourged him in the prison court. They thought they were the only ones who saw. But I saw. I dreamed. And what I saw I only partly understand. The soldiers' whips dismembered him and he lay, all his bones, upon the earth. Then there were only bones, white and scattered in a valley for as far as I could see. It was Ezekiel's prophecy. They were the bones of all the world and each of them a fragment of the body of my son. Among these bones I stood alone listening to the wind until the wind became a singing and the singing called my name. "Woman! Mary!" sang the wind among the bones. "Gather up these bones and make them whole." So I walked among the bones, gathering, connecting, fitting them together piece by piece. In my dream a thousand years passed by, and more, and I was old and I was gathering still.

These are days of dreaming when our souls see deeper than our eyes. These are times to trust the mysteries of heart that cannot be explained. I have heard that Pilate's wife dreams too. Her dreams hold warnings for the man who holds her body in the night. Dreams come, these days, through women and the men must heed. I met her once. She had veiled her face to not be recognized and stood back from the edges of the crowd. I felt her hungry listening. I drew near and took her hand; she looked at me. She removed her veil.

The days when I can hold my son are gone. Protection ceased to be a gift that I could give the day he walked from Nazareth to speak his name to all the world. Jesus—one who saves. He will not save himself. The world is pulling him apart as it is pulled. The world is stripping him because the world is split. We do to him exactly what is in our souls.

Mary with the face of beauty grasps my hand. She questions me. The ocean fills her eyes. "He is a leper," Mary gasps, "there is no place on him that is whole. Now is the end of beauty and of love. Insanity has gobbled up the world." I take her in my arms, the chosen sister of my son. Women, I can hold, for we have traded blood in bonds that birth new worlds. Our common blood consoles us in our grief.

Mary calls me mother. I remember years ago when Jesus was a boy and helping Joseph in the shop, I longed to birth a girl. I never did. Jesus called them sister, all the girls who came to me, some of them to live because their parents died before their time. My daughters circled me; I taught them how to spin and weave and tell the time of day from shadows cast on stone. I told with joy the mysteries of blood and birth and love that joins the body with the soul. I opened up my heart. They are my daughters still, and more come every day. Today my son goes out to meet his destiny. My daughters who have heard and loved his word, today begin to spin and weave the fibers of his dreams.

Those years we walked the countryside and hills of Lea's and her sister Rachel's sons, so many torn children of our land pleaded for a word, a touch, a blessing that would heal. The minds of some were torn in two and pain that scattered sanity poured from their mouths in a vomit of curses. Others could not walk, or could not hear, or see, or speak. There was a woman who had bled for years and could not leave her house without a curse because she was unclean. She could not bear a child because her womb was torn and would not hold a seed, nor could a seed be planted in a vessel that the law proclaimed unclean. For shame! Jesus healed them all. Now he stands torn by the sin that tore the world. He healed them all. I will remember as I share his pain with him; he healed them all.

Some of my daughters say the world of men is cursed. They say that it is time to return to the Mother only; abandon Yahweh and return. I say no! This is not the time for further severing. This is the time to join. Our God is one. Mother-Father God is one. Yahweh and Shekhinah, they are one. Even Anath, even Mara, even foreign Gods, they all are one. We divide ourselves. Now is the time for gathering. I tell them of my dream of bones.

°O∘O∘O°

A shout is rising up among the crowd. Blood is on their tongues. They want him dead. They want him crucified. The sound thunders and is shrill, it rolls and rises and it echoes off the Roman walls and down the corridors of power. It will not be still until he dies. Jesus stands broken in his blood and mirrors the truth of all our lives. The world will not hear the truth. The world will not see. The mourning in me rises to a wail. My daughters keen with me. Our sound is lost amidst the thunder of the crowd. We are chaos. We are the original depths. We are the cry over the waters.

°O∘O∘O°

I am old. My hair is white and all my skin folds upon itself like leather that is stretched. The tearing of my son disfigures me. This day I have seen too much; I will go blind. I open up my mouth to scream and make no sound. I am a cavern of pain. I am a pool of blood turned black. My fingers are bone. I tangle them into my coarse white hair and pull. I tear my veil and let it drop upon the stones. I fall to my knees. I put my forehead to the ground.

Glory that we can endure. Glory in the gathering of all that's torn, broken, scattered with the wind. Glory when there's nothing left but pain and yet we still go on.

CROWNS OF LIFE

THE THIRD SORROWFUL MYSTERY

THE CROWNING WITH THORNS

°O°O°O°

The Woman Speaks

Mother of mysteries, my head aches. So much to do. So much to figure out. I must remember and I must forget. I get confused. My head is circled with pain. My head feels ready to explode. I wanted to bring forth something out of my life, something worthy. I hoped to bring forth children of my heart, children of my mind, children of my womb. I feel so barren now. And I am old. My hair is turning gray. My face is lined. My years are written on my face. My children are lost. Gone from me. My children are not mine. Every child gives birth to itself. I am not needed. Thoughts of my lost children circle my head, they press in like a too-tight crown.

Mother Wisdom Speaks

I will wrap your children around your head like stars.
I will make them every color.
I will see them shine.
I will wrap your children around your life like water, like oceans,
   like currents, like a flow that never ends.

Your children will be the light that shines in the darkness.
Your children will stretch out into the universe.
They will hold hands.
They will laugh and they will fly.
They will walk between worlds.
They will be enormously beautiful.
They will be the children of forever.
They will be never-ending.

Your children will rise from the top of your head, streams of light,
    singing.
They are the melody of creation.
Your children can never be lost.
They will lead you by the hand.
They will open your heart.
They will open the future.
They will be your present, rejoicing.

They will make you soft.
You shall become soft as deep sand.
Your eyes as soft as a star-filled night.
Your smile soft as dew.
There will be nothing in your eyes that hurts.
You will be called healer.
You will be known as healer-mother.
And the children will spiral out from you,
Rising from the top of your head like light.
Your children will be light.
Your children will be the hopes of tomorrow.
Your children will love.

Your children will seek you for the softness.
You will no longer need to be right.
You will no longer strive to control life.
You will be soft.
You will let life be.
You will be life.

Do not despair.
The children are, right now, spiraling forth from you.
The children are dancing in the sky.
The children are circling the earth and renewing it.
They are mating with plants and trees.
They are growing trees within them.
They are the womb of tomorrow.
Your children are your love beyond its own power.
Your children will not die.

Do not fear.
Your children are, right now, laughing with the sound of all the
    waters of the world.
They are coming down like rain.
They are kissing the grass and making it grow.
They are the swirling tides.
They kiss the sand, the soft sand, the sand like glass, transformed.
Your children are the kiss that melts.
They are the fire turning the sands to molten glass.
They are the transformation.
They are crystal.
Your children shine.
They vibrate.
They are full of energy.

They are the transformation of the world.
Your children rise.

Be peaceful.
Be open.
The children are spiraling from the top of your head with laughter
  and with joy.
Your children are the renewal of the earth.

Mary Speaks

Abba, crown of love, compassionate, gentle yearning for life in
the not yet born, powerful flood of light within creation everywhere, only king, forever I've surrendered to your law. King of
tears, I watched Joseph lean into your whispered call and die; I
gave him freely, dancing the wonder of your rule that gives and
calls and gives again, a blessing both, receiving and the letting go.
King of destiny, we are your breath, the beating of your heart. We
live and die but you go on. You are the law of life. But this law
that mocks my son is not your law. This jealousy that crowns my
son with thorns will tear the world in two. This judgment shrivels
at the coward's hiss; it turns to lies; it murders love.

Thorns grew over a rock wall behind my girlhood home, vines
of thorns that made a barrier between us and the world. I thought
the thorns were beautiful at every time of year. In spring the vines
grew tiny leaves the shape of hearts and of a color nearly red and
delicately thin so that the light shone through. In summer, flow-

ers grew, small deep-throated five-petalled white with just a shadow of the palest rose. In fall the color fell away and through the
winter thorny tangles glinted in the slanted sun. The thorns
seemed polished by some careful woman who must tend the
earth to keep it fit. I marvelled at her work. I blessed the beauty
mingling fragility with power.

Who planted the thorns that grow against the prison wall?
Who gathered them? Who plaited them into a crown? Who
crushed them down onto the head and brow of him who is the
only one in all the world worthy to be called a king? Who twisted
beauty to devise such ugliness? Who dishonored earth and dese-
crated God?

The sight of my son quiets me. My daughter Mary screams. I
hear no weakness in her cry. Mary is a hawk, a wolf, a lion brave
before the one who kills from cowardice. Her heart is wild with
innocence; she has no fear of death. She fears treachery and so
she sees the truth. Mary sees they crowned him with their lies;
they pressed betrayal down; they pierced his soul.

All kingship of this world must kneel today. Even kings whose
hearts are pure remove their crowns. They lay them on the
ground. They return them to the earth. They melt the gold and
pour it through a fissure at the mountain's top. They cleanse

themselves of domination. They give it up. They plant their jewels. The rubies will spring up compassion and the sapphires, joy. Emeralds bring forth health; diamonds burst in song; amber gives a balm of peace; pearls gleam an iridescent hope around the pain of all the world.

No one notices us women as we leave the court of Pilate's shame. We pass a blind man at the gate who reaches out his hand. "Old man," Johanna whispers as she bends to him, "we have no gift today. The gift that we were born to give is cast aside and mocked. Praise God you cannot see what we have seen." I touch him as we pass because he seems to me the image of the world.

While we waited at the house of Salome I fell into a fitful sleep. I dreamed I came into the temple through the gate called Beautiful. I thought that I was coming home and had three days to choose if I would stay. I yearned to want to stay but I could not. From outside its walls the temple still looked strong, but decay weakened it within. The high priest stood in tattered robes and the phylacteries he wore were frayed. His tarnished breastplate was devoid of jewels and his eyes were filled with scorn. He stood as if to guard the place called Holy. He raised his hand. He raised his palm against me. He stood before the temple veil, under the golden crown of the holiest place, and he kept me out. I reached my hand to him. He, too, is my son.

It was then I saw the fire. Fire licked along the floor. Fire crackled at the crown of each acacia pillar circling the holy place. Fire ringed the tattered hem of the robe the high priest wore and then it caught the veil. The veil of separation behind which God was said to sit fell in a mighty roar of flame. I stood amazed. I prayed the fire might reveal the presence of our God transplendent on his throne. Charred acacia wood was all I saw. The throne is in our hearts. The temple fire is purifying souls.

I woke and knew I am the fire. I am woman whose body became flesh for God. The temples are ourselves. We are the crown of flame.

I woke and John was holding me. "It's gone." With my spirit I could feel the pulse of the world's heart and it was being purified. "All worldly domination's gone; all illusions of separation, gone; and all the laws by which we claimed false power—-all are gone. We stand at the edge of night and all the kings and all the priests have bowed their heads and we are left alone with just my son to show the way, my son, crowned with thorns. I taste the ashes of a world's ending on my tongue and yet I cry to Adonai, the gate of life, crown of the womb, to bring us through. I seek the wandering Shekhinah who, in exile, wears a crown of tears. I yearn for Hokmah, womb circling the world, to give us birth. And all the sons and daughters of the earth seem to circle round my own head like a crown of stars."

I rise now and I go alone to where my son will pass and then I'll walk with him as I have always done and I will be there when he dies. This world has passed and we are in between. The mid-morning air is without wind and sunlight bakes the stones beneath my feet. My heart is crowned with flames.

°O∘O∘O°

Glory in the truth unveiled. Glory in the one who stands against all lies. Glory in the alchemy that transforms worlds. Glory in the crown of fire.

GREEN WOOD

THE FOURTH SORROWFUL MYSTERY

THE CARRYING OF THE CROSS

The Woman Speaks

Mother of mysteries, the times are hard for sons. They are the green wood in a drought. These days the earth quakes and mountains start to fall. It is time for the scape of our inner land to change, for wood dried in the long heat of sun to be covered by the hills so the ground can once again yield green.

We women reach out our hands in supplication for the one whose heart is green. He will unite the divided ones. He will free those who cling to small certainties. He will keep his peace when taunted by those still blind to innocence. His being is his proof. His spirit's moist and growing. The wood of sin is dry.

What begins as the son's dream, we mothers bear into wakefulness. The mother carries the dream past death, through places and through times of dream distortion; she carries the dream in her womanhood; she carries it down all the pathways of the world and she grows large with the dream and yet it is not born.

Mother, each woman is a refugee from many wars. She has walked all the roads and there is nothing that she has not seen. Horror haunts her eyes. She is unnoticed by the rulers and the priests. She sits beside a wall in the city and feels the dream grow. She lies down under a flowering tree in the field and feels the dream grow. She thinks that she will burst with it but the world does not see how big she is, how ripe.

The woman's hair turns gray. Her face and hands are the bark of an oak. She wonders if the dream is stuck in her, if she will die with it. The dream is a cross lodged in her soul and will not be moved. She is carrying the cross and no one sees. The mother carries the cross to the end of the world and crouches there. There she will await the quaking of earth. Our world sees her there and thinks she is a tree covered with moss. But she is danger. She is the tumbling of mountains and the falling of hills.

Mother Wisdom Speaks

I know that you don't want to die.
I know your heart.
I call from your heart with the voice of blood.
I call in the beating of your heart.
I call you my daughter.
I call all my sons.
I am the heart beating.
I am the blood.
I am life and all that rushes forward into a new world.

Listen.
You are my body.
This is the death you feel.
This is the transformation.
I am preparing you.
I am making you ready.
You are she who walks on mountains.
You are the woman waiting at the edge of a crevasse.

You are the mother straining to give birth.
You are the tree.
You are the sentinel.

I know that you don't want to die.
Each breath is death.
Each blinking of your eye.
Each heartbeat.
And each is life.
It is a passage.
A way.

Daughter, give your heart away.
Love.
Write this: Do not be afraid.
Open up your heart.
Open and they will come to you, you will feel them like drops of
    rain, you will feel their fluttering like the wings of birds.
They are the daughters and the sons.
Open up to them.
Let no one be excluded.
You are the way home.

Take courage.
You are my body.
Within you my own heart beats.
Write this.
You are like a box.
Treasure is stored in you.
Open the lid.
You are a rosewood box.

You contain love letters.
You are filled with shells.
Dried rose petals.
Stalks of wheat thousands of years old.
Keep the box open.

You are the road coming home.
You are the box.
You are filled with food.
Keep open.
My people will want to eat from you.
You are a box at the end of the road.
You are full of dreams.
They are my dreams.
They will come true.

You are my body.
There is no pain that is not everybody's pain.
There is no longing that does not belong to all.
There is one dream.
All my children want to come home.
Everyone will walk this road.

Mary Speaks

Abba, we stand against the world's edge and beyond is nothing we can see. This is the step into hell. Thick night closes round. We sink through primal waters impervious to light. Chaos dissolves us. We will be nothing again. We do not choose this way; it is the only road. All our lifetime led us here. The only way through death is death itself.

I wait here by the wall. I wait where the gate is closed against the shouts of soldiers who prepare the crossbeam for my son. I wait in the silence of God.

The heavy wooden door grates against the stones and opens to expose my son. I see his eyes. They are the only part of him I recognize; the rest is blood and a body stretched, straining under wood. I see his eyes and he sees mine and we are one. I stand. My bones are granite; I can walk this way with him. I enter through his eyes and span his soul. I am his mother. Once I sheltered him beneath my heart and fashioned from my breath and bone this body that he wears. Now I enter him to bear the weight, to be firm earth beneath his striving. We will walk this way as one. My mind is diamond. Together we endure.

Once on the road to Naim we walked and wept with villagers whose keening and whose drums announced a death—a widow's only son. I walked beside her and she leaned on me as if she knew our destinies entwined. That day, like this one, scorched our throats as we drew breath and dried our wails into a locust cry. The widow smelled like dust stirred up from centuries of lying stale on earth without rain. Her veils brushed against me like the ancient webs of spiders that have died. She was what I might be without dreams. And I remember her today. Mercy rained upon her dry heart. Compassion restored her son.

°O°O°O°

My son falls. The soldiers hold me off. I am pressed behind a crush of people from the countryside. I cannot move. Someone rips away my veil; my cloak is torn. I can no longer see him where he lies; I cannot help. My heart is stone ground down. I feel his weakness in my soul. "Make way, old woman," shouts a soldier as he pushes me into a wall and down upon my knees. My head is bent. My blood seeps to the ground.

°O°O°O°

"Mother, you are ill; here, take my arm." A man with onyx eyes and voice like midnight waves upon the Sea of Galilee is lifting me. Oh, and he is strong. He is the stranger of the way. "Once there was a man," I say, "who on the road between Jerusalem and Jericho, fell in with thieves. They beat him and they left him nearly dead. You are the same as he who came to care for him."

"No, Mother, you are wrong. I am from Cyrene."

I was not wrong. This and the other road are one. Those who lie wounded are my son. The stranger of the way will always come.

°O°O°O°

In Jerusalem today the women weep. They see what happens to our sons. Which child of which young woman here will walk this

same road thirty years from now when she is old and cannot bear
another? Whose sons in all the centuries to come will suffer
under those who fear to lose their power and every gift of earth
they claim to own? Which daughters of the women crying here
will spend their lives in fear for children they might bear? We
women know. Whoever sets upon this road carries either
weapons or a cross. This is the road of war. This is the road of
greed. This is the road of domination. This road is dry as the
souls of those who paved its way. This road leads to the world's
end.

I call her Veronica. Whether she was flesh and blood or was an
angel I don't know. I saw her only when she left the crowd. The
soldiers' horses reared and almost trampled her but she was not
deterred. Perhaps time stopped; I thought I heard the wind and
all the shouts were stilled. The woman, who was neither young
nor old, wore a saffron dress covered by a violet cloak and veil of
white. Summoning a soldier for his water flask, she removed her
veil and wet it on the edge. From Jesus's face the woman washed
the blood. She took her time. Later on she found me in the
crowd. "Mother, take this gift of vera iconica, from your son."
The woman pressed her folded veil into my arms. I opened it to
find imprinted the "true image" of my son.

Just so his image is on all our lives. Look in the eyes of the man
born blind; you will see Veronica. Dance with Jarius's daughter
who had died and lives today because of him and you are dancing

with Veronica. The woman from Samaria—Veronica. The little ones who listened when he spoke and climbed up on his lap and told their secrets in his ears—Veronica. All his friends who followed him these years, the rich young man who went away, Zachias in the sycamore, the centurion whose son was ill, Simeon of the Pharisees whom he taught of love, all of these and more— Veronica. Each veils his face, as does the earth on which he walked, as does the sky he loved. Each, if it is opened up, reveals the truth of him.

He is what we've come to know is God, and yet he falls. And yet he falls again. Can we then kill God? Now that I am old and I have seen what I have seen, I think we can. We can kill God both in our world and in our souls. When we kill the best of what we are, we kill our future and our dreams.

We have reached the summit of the Mount of Skulls. We cover our faces with cloth to filter the stench of the unburied dead. They strip him so we see the lacerations of the whip. My tears come now to find that all the beauty of our hope is gone. The women who are with me hide their eyes, but I do not hide. This is my son. His is the body of our dreams.

I will dry my tears. I will stand and I will not cry out. I will not trust the violent with my pain. Once I thought myself daughter of

Hokmah, image of Shekhinah, the wisdom of our God to have given birth to such a son; now I know that I am not. There is no wisdom left in all the earth. The rape of man has driven her away to wander with the not-yet-born. I thought I heard the angels at his birth. On this mountaintop of skulls the angels never sing. And this is where my son will die. And I, a common woman, will receive his dreams with his last breath. And then this world will end. But I, I will go on.

Glory when we're stripped of every hope. Glory in our striving all our life and dying distant from our dreams. Glory in the darkest night. Glory in the cave beneath the steepest mountain of the earth. And when we think that even God has died, glory in the faith that cries: I will go on.

REVEAL, AWAKEN, REMEMBER

THE FIFTH SORROWFUL MYSTERY

THE CRUCIFIXION AND DEATH OF JESUS

The Woman Speaks

Mother of mysteries, death, like birth, is your mystery. It is the great round, the cycle of being. Even in violent death you are there, standing amid the skulls. You are the promise of continuing life.

You are the revealer. You destroy lies. You obliterate our resistance to reality. You wipe away our denials. You open our eyes to the consequences of every sin: domination, egoism, possessiveness, greed, duplicity, deliberate thoughtlessness, all of which result in violence and finally violent death, to our spirits first of all, and then to everything. You look on the crucified one. You reveal what we have done.

You are the awakener. You bring hope. You restore our spirits and our lives. You quicken us again within your womb. You are the one who knows that death is not the end. You raise up the dead to life. You awaken our bodies and our minds. You inspire us with technologies to restore the earth we have poisoned with waste and decimated with war.

You are the rememberer. You teach contemplation. You are the priest who bakes the bread and serves the wine and tells the story of the human God who died because of what forgetfulness can do. You warn us never to forget.

You are the Mother. You bear the memory of death in your soul
and the seed of life in your heart. You do not abandon us. You
birth us always new. You are the quaking earth.

Mother Wisdom Speaks

This is death.
This is the edge, the fine slash in the heart.
This is where you stand.
This is the moment of cutting through, the moment of the blade.
See me.
I stand at the intersection.
I stand where two worlds meet.
I am the crimson light.
I am the moon bathed in blood.
I am the catch in your breath.
I am the pause between.
I am the rattling of your release.
I am the mercy of release.

I am the soft red of sunset.
I am the searing red of spilled blood.
I am the still white of the abandoned body,
The body turned to earth,
The elemental body, matter.
Mater.
I stand at the edge in billowing gowns.
Veils like storm clouds.
I am the light.
Reach for me.

Walk into me.
I am what beckons.
I am the quickening.
I am the drawing of your heart.
I am the voice, calling.
I am the smile.
You see me vaguely, then more clearly as you come.

I am the golden cup.
I am silver rings that intersect.
I am all time.
I am every tomorrow of which you dreamed.
I am the warmth into which you pass.
I am the light towards which you are drawn,

Like a seed on the wind, like breath,
I breathe you into me.
I take you into my heart.
I sing to you.
You hear my song and you know it is your life.
I give you your life.
I give you all you've ever desired truly.

I kiss your every wound.
I heal the tear in your soul.
I heal your death.

I wrap you round with mystery.
I wind you in mysteries as in a soft web.
I wrap you in my shawl.
It is the morning.

It is the dawn of a new world.
I fill your feet with dancing and your throat with song.
I set you on tiptoe in the clouds.
You dance with my stars.
You sing and the heavens ring so sweetly hearts all over the earth
  break open.
Love floods the barren land.
The earth turns green.
The earth shivers with delight.

I sing with you.
I am your song.
Now there is no distance between us.
You are home.
You have died into my body.
You are transformed.
You are alive, and you are home.

Mary Speaks

Abba, he called on you and I will hear his cry for all my life. He called and he received the silence of the darkened sun. You have no power here, on Golgotha; you still are love and this death is not your will. You could not save him. You are what the sinful world would kill. He is your Word; the world has silenced him. His hands bestowed your blessing; the world has nailed them to the cross. His feet walked the way of truth; the world has nailed them to the cross. You loved us with his heart; the world has pierced him with a lance. Abba, this is not your work; it is the work of fear, the work of anger and of the imprisoned heart.

°O°O°O°

Should I be howling like a she-wolf of the hills whose lair is gutted and whose young are scattered dead upon the rocks? Should I let loose the cry tearing at my throat with claws? Behind me from the women in the crowd keening rises into the dark sky like the scream of eagles. But I hold my keening down. I close my lips against knives of sound sheering my soul. The Word has died. Nothing I can say is strong enough.

°O°O°O°

I am no longer soft. They loose him from the tree and lay him on my lap and I am stone. I am the insensible mountain. I am the ancient volcano that is cold. Within me crawl the little cleansing worms, polishing my bones, obsidian and diamond, preparing me to bear this load of death. He, too, is bone. Death makes one thing of us. Neither of us feels the rain.

°O°O°O°

Where are the angels now? Thunder ate them. Sky vomited them out into the gaping maw of earth that closed and crushed them, silencing their songs of peace. The angels were a dream but now the violence of man has wakened me. I hold my dream and he is dead. The wings of angels ceased to beat when my son's heart stilled.

°O°O°O°

My eyes are caves. You who make laws to bind the women's hands and feet, you cannot travel there, it is too dark. I would let you, but you are afraid and so you laugh and say that I am nothing anyway. Your laughter is a jackal in the night. You tear at life with sharp teeth. You hide our food. You stand before the gaping holes that were my eyes and laugh.

The veil is torn. The secrets of the temple lie exposed, raped and torn by faithlessness. The rulers' rods break. The priest is freed from temple walls. The priest is here, at Golgotha. We are the sacrifice and gift. We are the way. The priest of God drinks from the cup and descends through the dark cave. The priest joins earth to sky. The priest is the tree. The priest is caldron and is fire. The priest is bread and she whose flesh is flour. The priest is chalice and is wine. I, who am granite and whose eyes are caves, I am the priest with him whose life flows through me into God.

I thought I was alone. Myself, the body of my son, and rain. The others, Salome, John, the Magdalene, seemed ghosts against the coming night. But multitudes come singing up the mountainside. Sarah and Abraham, holding hands. And Rebecca, Isaac and their sons. Rachel, Lea, all the tribes. Joseph of Egypt with the foreign Gods like lights around his head. Miriam is dancing around Moses with his hair aflame. Ruth brings wheat and Esther brings a crown. They bow. And all the world bows. I am filled with graciousness. I am a queen. From the treasure on my lap I bestow on them the Gift of Life.

°O∘O∘O°

Time frees us from its bonds. I still am still and Jesus still is dead but death is like a dream. Rain falls but we are dancing in the sun. The cross that was so bloody towers to the sky. I cannot see its top. It is a flowering tree. Adam dances there with Eve and Lilith laughing, drinking from a stream with seven branches rushing out to water all the world. Then Jesus rises from my lap and he invites me to the dance. We whirl round the tree. We are light. Sparks fly from us and become angels that are stars shining beside the sun at noon.

°O∘O∘O°

John touches me. "Mother," he whispers with the sound of tears, "Mother, it is time." I raise my head to the rain.

°O∘O∘O°

Rain cleansed him of blood and grime. Salome brings herbs and lays them on his wounds. She prays. "Reveal!" I can be glad of this: he never faltered from truth. He lived truth's passion and died in its embrace. He did not deny his name. The Magdalene anoints him with perfume. She prays "Awake!" She prays it for the world. The other Mary covers him with ointment that preserves and prays "Remember!" This prayer seals our hearts. It makes us who we are. Then John winds the cloths around him and we carry him away.

°O∘O∘O°

I am the mother. I am the tomb. I will bring him forth again. I am earth. In the silent darkness of my body's cave he waits. He is seed. He will blossom when the moon is full. He is fire and he will flame forth.

Glory in the earth who holds us all. Glory for the gift both offered and received. Glory in the dreams that will not die.

MYSTERIES OF GLORY

Wherever I look

Let me see that all is one

Let me open my heart

As a channel for divine compassion

I completed the mysteries of sorrow as the February days became longer and the sun shone with less slant upon the hills. Then I could not write. At first I saw no reason for concern over my emptiness. I know the rhythms of creation. My husband, John, and I drove down the coast to refresh ourselves.

Half way we found Big Sur Lodge. We arrived about four in the afternoon, got our cabin, parked the car and before unloading we went for a walk in the mountainous woods. We walked until sunset: first up a steep path to Lookout Point from which we could see peak upon peak and valley within valley. Beyond the hills the ocean gleamed where Point Sur stood against the surf.

I got so winded climbing that my heart beat in my ears. We came down past a tall, thin waterfall that helps to create the Big Sur river. We entered the redwood groves. They are a holy place. Among them we are dwarfed, more than in a cathedral. At this time of year all the new evergreen shoots are flowering, filtering the setting sun where it beams down through the tall spires. The ground is clear of weeds, like the ground under the Minnesota pines of my childhood where rust-colored needles make a soft bed. But here the bed is thicker, softer. I hold my breath.

At night we built a fire and read aloud to each other. After breakfast we went on another walk before we left for San Simeon, this time along the Big Sur River, clear mountain water that gurgles over rocks and hides rainbow trout in deep hollows. Leaf buds decorated the aspens that lean over the stream.

In San Simeon our room was ground level with a little patio, a space of grass, and then a twenty-five foot bluff that dropped off to the beach. Nothing but ocean in front of us and the constant sound of surf. At night we dreamed of waves. We lit a fire in the fireplace and lay in bed surrounded by ocean and the flicker of firelight. We spent four nights there. During the days we walked the beach. We contemplated the mysteries of tidal pools in bowls carved by the sea from rock. Farther down, the ocean washes jade pebbles onto the sand. We bent and picked up jewels.

The day following our return I sat down to write of glory. Emptiness. I waited. I didn't know what for. On the Vernal Equinox the words began to come.

I almost failed to make the connection. I said to John over morning coffee "If sorrow is an earthquake, what is glory?"

"Sunsets are always glorious," he replied a bit distractedly.

"Yes, and dawn...."

Of course. Glory: the splendor of balance in wholeness. Opposites meet and become one in dawn, in dusk—day and night in perfect balance, for a moment neither day nor night but both. The equinox, too, is a balance of opposites. Equal light, equal darkness, the Easter moment.

The mysteries of wholeness, the mysteries of wisdom, are the mysteries of opposites wed to one another. "The one who died is alive!" cry the astonished followers of Jesus. Any glorious mystery astonishes us.

Glory is the realm of miracle. Here we are transformed; our perspective shifts and expands. Suddenly the world becomes transparent and we see through the surface of things into their living soul. What had seemed separate on the surface is connected within. What seemed dead, lives. What seemed lost is present on a parallel plane of reality. A spirit inhabits creation and breathes our being full of glory. We enter these mysteries awestricken. They explode our minds and hearts; we burst with light. We grasp for words to describe what we have entered and we stammer "resurrection" and "ascension;" we cry "alleluia!"

Glory, absolutely present in our lives but obscured by our mundane endeavors, can burst out, unexpected, at any time through anything. You can be walking along, minding your business, headed to work maybe, or taking the children to the park when suddenly, splendor. These are moments of truth when who you are and what you do become not only clear but brilliant. You perceive the miracle in existence and you glory in it. The miracle, the splendor, the brilliance, the glory erupt with more than human being so much that you stand awed in the being of the holy.

The mystery of glory frees us from the structure of space and time we have created to give order to our worlds, and opens us to eternity, the unity of the soul with love, the perfect connectedness of all creation with itself and of itself with the Godheart. Glory is the overflow of God's spirit, the stuff of which we are made. Glory is the transplendence of divine love.

Glory is the gift, both the blessing and the thanks. Glory is a circle of love never-ending. We receive what is God into our deepest selves and by receiving we return ourselves as gift to God who is our beginning. Each life and the combined life of the cosmic world enacts the gift of glory.

The God of glory transcends image and gender by circling and penetrating to their depths. Our breakthrough into glorious mystery brings us beyond comprehensibility of any human faculty— reason, emotion or imagination—into pure being and infinite existence in which all exists in unity. Beyond father and beyond mother because completely and non-exclusively both father and mother in wholeness. The Hebrews of the Exodus identified glory with the Shekhinah of God, that presence of fire guiding them through the day and the same presence in cloud with them throughout the night. Yahweh's presence among them was a divine feminine presence and they experienced no contradiction in this. These are the mysteries of the soul. Whether or not actual historical events in the life of Jesus led his followers to proclaim belief in a mystery of resurrection, the mystery itself is a miracle of the soul. So also are the other glorious mysteries miracles of the soul. Human experiences often trigger the event, but the mystery happens on another plane of being altogether. We cannot prove the glory. We cannot give evidence of miracle. We cannot explain mystery. The transformation of glory belongs within the sphere of faith.

Faith's sphere is dark. The necessity that light has for darkness evokes wonder. We marvel. Here we see mystery in the obvious. Paradox. In our souls we discover that from the moist oozing darkness life springs. In the night of unknowing awakens the purest Truth.

But these are images—darkness, light, earth—all images for something too deep to imagine. But without images we cannot re-present any experience, so we are compelled to use them— words, pictures, music, dance—and all of them are as illusory as they are true. The difference between the non-believer and the believer is that when all illusions are dissolved what remains is either a barren void or glory.

Any experience of the glorious mystery—always timeless, simultaneously fleeting and eternal and spaceless, more full that any image—brings us immediately back to earth, embodiedness, incarnation. Glorious mystery which is transcendent and of the future nevertheless roots us securely in the present earth of our time/space existence. The glorious touch of infinite love transforms us into compassion. The participation in absolute unity transforms all our relationships and creates in us a realization of connections. We become an incarnate and conscious outpouring of divine love. This incarnate consciousness is the essence of Christ and the body of the Mother.

Rising from death, transforming creation, opening to the spirit, embracing the rejected, uniting with divine love: these are the mysteries of glory. All awaken us to what we are. All proclaim connections of creation with the divine Mother, wisdom. These mysteries poise us where the edges of opposite realities meet and meld, where we feel the keen tension of standing in two worlds at once and the ecstacy of their joining. We celebrate them in our daily lives, in choices large and small. We celebrate them each according to our willingness to take our place as one with, continuous with, everything created. Many times this willingness requires that we be "reduced" to earth, to remember that "we are dust." Death of loved ones, loss of hopes, failure to live up to ideals, limits of our talents or courage or endurance, and in these present times the rape of earth, the pollution of our air, the holes torn in our atmosphere, our lethal wastes, our willingness to resort to war—all bring us to our knees and foster in us empathy with all that is. All creation breathes as one. We live or die together.

The grace of these glorious mysteries is that each of us, like Mary, finds the holy in herself. "The day of my spiritual awakening," says Mechtilde of Magdeburg, "is the day I saw and knew that I saw, all things in God and God in all things."[6]

"When the sun rests on the horizon, watch." John and I sat on our motel patio overlooking the Pacific at sunset. "When it sinks below the water you'll see a flash of green in the red sky. It's only there an instant. It's easy to miss." We watched the western sky at the edge of our earth for this miracle of opposites. At the moment of balance, when day and night combined, we saw the wonder.

"Aren't sunsets glorious?" John smiled and took my hand.

A Reborn World

The First Glorious Mystery

The Resurrection

The Woman Speaks

Mother of mysteries, I remember women. Women singing "Resurrexit" high in the loft of the small knotty pine church in Baudette, Minnesota. Women making Easter breads and coloring Easter eggs. Women cleaning house because it was the time of year for all things to be new. Women finding something green in the just melted Minnesota land—usually pussy willows that they brought to the house two weeks ahead of time and put in warm water to open their buds by Easter day. Sometimes it snowed when the full moon followed close after the Vernal Equinox thus placing Easter toward the end of March, but even then my mother wore flowers in her hair.

When I was fifteen we went home after the Easter Vigil and my mother and I hid Easter eggs for my little sister, Betsy, to find the next morning. We laughed to imagine her delight in discovering such wonders in such ordinary places. Although we didn't think it out, the ritual of the Easter Vigil and the family tradition of hiding the decorated eggs are connected. We are women, accustomed to experiencing miracle in the most simple things of life.

Life rises with a subtleness easy to miss; and even if we sense the rising it is easy to deny. Everything we see and hear and feel we could interpret in another way. The man who came to Mary

Magdalene in the garden didn't look like Jesus; she thought he was the gardener. But there was something in his voice, a slight lifting on the first syllable of her name perhaps, that touched her heart so that she trusted her response and she believed in him. Or those who walked the road to Emmaus thought he was a stranger to the land. Then they "recognized him in the breaking of the bread." Simple. Subtle. Not hard proof, certainly. Anyone can break bread. But a barely perceptible difference in the way he bent his head or how he paused a moment over the loaf, and they saw him there.

This is women's language. A catch of breath. A lifting of the eyes. A language of gardening and baking bread. Touch and the withholding of touch. The petal of a flower sent only with her name. "Read between the lines," my mother used to say. She meant explore the space around the news of daily things and feel it as a heart-beat. Resurrection speaks with women's language. The mother tongue. The women spread the news.

Mother of mysteries, I am listening; I want to hear your voice.

Mother Wisdom Speaks

Take your right hand to your heart,
To the center where your heart beats,
To the place between your breasts,
The hollow place,
The place where you protect pain.
Touch your heart.
Let your fingers press on that place.
Let it open.
Let the heart open under the pressure of your fingers.
Let there be a flowering in your heart.

Let it be a lotus.
Let it be a rose.
Let the emptiness open into a flower.
Let the dead arise.
Let the closed be open.
Let the seed burst forth.

Out of you comes sweetness.
Out of you the scent of roses.
Out of you the pure lily-scent.
Out of you the heavy full scent of life.
It is simple.
Just open.
The tomb, open.
The womb, open.
The heart, open fully.
Let your heart be a pathway.
Let the poor come into you.
Let there be love.
Let your heart be the essence of loving kindness.
This is the resurrection.
This is the transformation.
This is the mystery that is my name.
Other than this, beyond this there is nothing further towards
   which you must strive.
And do not strive for this.
Simply open your heart.

If anyone has hurt you, forgive that one.
Do it simply.
Forgiveness is the balm of love.

Your own forgiveness heals your own wounds.
In forgiving your brothers and your sisters you are forgiven.
Open up your heart.
This is resurrection.

Let your heart sing.
Let your heart be free.
After this opening fear is gone.
Life is all there is.
Eternal life.
This is peace.
This is the essence of peace.
Your self, forgiven.
Everyone will enter through your open heart.
Death broke open your heart like a husk.
Your need for protection is past.
Love will be your protection.
Love makes you clear.
You can say no.
You can say yes.
Either one.
Both of them you will say with love.

You are the flowering tree.
You are the soaring song.
You are the open door.
You are the flower that does not fade.
You are my heart.
You are the heart of my love.
Feel the beat of your heart.
Press your fingers gently on that living beat.

Open your heart.
This is your Easter.
This is your resurrection.
This is the resurrection of the earth, of all the living.
This is the watering of what you thought dead.
I am a stream of water within you.
Open your heart.
I will flood the barren plain.
I will be a waterfall on the mountain.
I will be the ocean at full tide.
I will rise in you, so wet, so nourishing, so complete.
I will make everything grow.
I will turn the earth green.
I will make green your heart.
Green light will shine around you.
Children will witness it.
And all those whose hearts have remained young.
They will laugh and their laughter will be bliss and it will make
    them whole.
They will come to you to stand inside your green light.

Out of your open heart life will flow.
I will flow from you.
This is your resurrection.
This is your joy.
This is bliss.
The fullness of every hope.
Fear dissolves in my bliss.
What is left to fear?
Everything is one.
All is part of the whole.

Love your enemy.
There is no enemy anymore.
The one you called enemy is part of you.
Live in that one.
Open your heart.
That one will live in you.
Together you will be transformed.
When one of you rise, all of you rise.
Easter is the transformation of the world.

Mary Speaks

I awoke at dawn. I waked the world with the opening of my eyes; I raised up the sun. I stretched my arms and touched encircling seas. My arms are wings, my breath the spirit of all life. From my vast womb the cosmos springs newborn. I open my mind to release the embodied Word. Dense earth explodes. Solid rock ignites and fire fills the land. My bones vibrate with the song of God. Shekhinah lives within me, found. The stars pour out of me with singing.

Where you are, Christed One, I am. I circle you like rainbows round the sun. We rise. A lark sings; we are song. We slept and dreamt we walked down roads where sharp stones cut our feet and we were not allowed to make a sound. We wore the face of death and made the journey to the womb of earth. There you lay three days while I poured out upon your soul the seven-fold balm of holiness. I circled you and danced the dance of life.

°O∘O∘O°

The mountain shudders and the stone rolls back. Deeper than my womb I feel a quickening more sharp than the life bond made when first you moved. This life is lightning blazing through my densest earth. Light streaks upward from my womb and through my heart. Light bursts in my throat and shines behind my eyes. My head is all ablaze. I sing. I wear the diadem of morning in my hair.

Your voice roars like oceans through my blood; you are here. You whisper in my mind like wind. John's mother made a garden in the courtyard of her home; I waited there. I sat where roses twined through rocks that once fit well to make a wall. In these three days a sparrow wove her nest. I saw her mirrored in the pool of my soul. I slept beneath the stars. The other women went with ointments to the tomb. I watched Venus rise beside the sun at dawn.

My daughter rang into the garden like a thousand golden bells. Her mourning robe that covered her these past three days was gone. She had undone her hair, put on her silver dancing dress and lapis beads. She looked nineteen-years-old, the morning of her wedding day. Mary threw her arms around my waist and raised her head. Her eyes swam into mine. "You've seen him, too," was all she said.

°O∘O∘O°

The others came more quietly, Salome, Joanna, Mary in whose home we stay; the men would not believe the angel's words, the women said. But Peter went to see, and John. My daughters sang the ancient cry of glory. Higher, higher rose the tone until our ululation rocked the air and birds and animals cried out and even all the cedars of the forests shouted joy. Alleluia! all the women sang. And Alleluia! echoed back all creatures who had ears to hear. We took hands then in the circle women make to celebrate Sophia who gives life and we began to dance, slowly, slowly first, swaying in and out, our bodies in a universal pulse of worlds circling, becoming without end; then faster, singing, chanting, whirling, howling Alleluia on the currents of the air, crying we would spread the news, laughing at the quickness of our steps that would not stop, that would not tire us because we knew the Christed One had risen from the dead, and we had risen too.

Many saw him; many were not sure. It took a certain kind of sight, a listening with the heart that feels its way toward truth. Those whose hearts were hard proclaimed it was not so and went away. Some returned. I sat spinning wool when Cleopas came to me. He burst into my afternoon with laughter and with tears. "We saw him, Mother, in a stranger's eyes. He walked with us. It was the time when sun and moon are balanced on the edge of earth, and day is nearly spent. We stopped to rest at Emmaus where we shared our bread with him. When he blessed the bread and broke it, that was when we saw! I whispered 'Rabbi,' and he smiled." Cleopas knelt and put his head upon my knees. "Forgive me, Mother, for my fear." And then he placed a bundle in my open hands. I untied the clean white cloth. Cleopas brought me bread, broken and blessed.

Amazed, they brought me stories, all my sons, how they saw him in the upper room and knew him by his wounds. Some of them saw brilliance where before there had been blood. They told me how he came to them at night when they were at sea and moonlight walked the waves. He walked with moonlight over the water. He built a fire on the rocky shore and fed them roasted fish at dawn. Some said he told them Peter would not die. John said that wasn't what he meant. They said he gave them power over life and death and called the power "forgiveness." My sons are drunk with him. He is shining in their eyes; he is reeling in their minds. I lay my hands upon their heads. I bless them. My daughters sing to give them strength. They are drinking from the cup. They have eaten the bread.

The world is newborn. I feel a rising in my heart of something more, something waiting to be seen and felt and known in everything. I recognize him in the singing of the thrush who sits upon her nest in grasses bunching up against the shore along the lake of Galilee. His is the breath by which I am alive, the rush of music through me as I bend and flow like willow branches dancing in the day. There is nothing where he does not live. And everywhere he is, I am and we are one.

°O∘O∘O°

He calls to me with ancient names. His word rings across the canopy of sky. His body is the universe unfolding like a flower at the tender kiss of dawn. His being blooms shimmering beneath the divine touch. And he calls me. He calls Hokmah and within my mind wings spread above the void; creation springs. He calls Shekhinah and I open wide my soul to make a home for God. He calls Sophia, wisdom sings in me, the universal song. He calls me Mary, common woman, mother of God.

I unfold. I let go my life. Worlds fall from me like stars.

You wonder how I know. I know. I am a simple woman in a garden on a common day, and yet I know. They come to me, these ordinary folk with stories of the miracle they sense and I can only say, I know. I make a circle with the women and we sing, we gossip some, we share our recipes for food and healing and we know, all of us, we know. He is alive. The dream goes on. We share the bread and wine. We hold each other's hands. We offer what we have. We speak the truth. We honor all of life. The new world is a simple one and it has come.

Glory in the rising sun, the circling days, the cycles of years, the whirling worlds. Glory in the ready heart and the receiving mind. Glory in eyes that see and ears that hear beyond what seems. Glory in all life made new.

Heaven Everywhere

The Second Glorious Mystery

The Ascension

The Woman Speaks

Mother of mysteries, I thought of heaven as a place until I was twenty-four years old. I still remember exactly where I was and what I was doing when some door in my mind opened and I perceived heaven as infinite presence. It was the eve of the Ascension in 1965. I sat at a typewriter in a classroom at St. Joseph's Academy in Crookston, Minnesota, reflecting on the coming feast-day. An image of the scriptural scene as presented by artists hovered in my mind. Jesus stood lightly on a cloud, his hands raised in blessing and his body surrounded by a halo of sunlight. I waited for my Jesus-image to ascend. But he didn't go up. Instead, his body began to shine and to become translucent. Then the light, which now he was, expanded to include and penetrate the earth and sky until there was nothing that was not suffused with him and everything existed within him who now had no limits. He had "ascended" into an unlimited dimension of reality. He became an infinite and eternal presence.

"Heaven is no-place and everywhere. The ascended Christ is the infinite and eternal dimension of all reality." Those are the words I typed that day when I was twenty-four years old and wondering what Ascension Day might mean.

Today is Earth Day. Environmentalists will march in the streets of San Francisco and other cities and towns throughout the nation. Dolphins will leap and call to one another off the California coast because the tuna nets in which they've tangled and died for years are banned. Outside the winds of April dance with the new leaves. This morning it rained, a celebration of hope this year of drought. I stood with my feet on the earth and my head in the sky and let my face be washed in miracle. We will see Christ coming in the same way that he went. Why not in the rain? Why not in the spring that bubbles up from earth at Lourdes or in Mendocino, or the Sierras, or beside a tumbled shed on a farm beside the Red River of the North? Why not in the plaintive song of the mourning dove who wakes me every day? Why not in the clasp of my sister's hand? Why not in her voice or in her body, more like mine that any other in this world? Why not in my husband's embrace? Why not in a stranger's smile? Why not in the ever-recurring spring. Why not in the renewing of the earth?

My husband, John, and I will plant a tree.

Mother Wisdom Speaks

I want you to believe me.
You are wider than you ever knew.
You are the world.
You have lived so long within the narrow borders of your mind,
    within the hard boundaries of your smallest self.
Expand.
Feel limitlessness.
There are no edges to the universe.
It beats within you.
Your flesh is air.

If you just let it go you can feel your spaciousness.
You will know that nothing keeps you from union.
There is no distance between you and everyone you love.
There is not distance at all.
Your illusion of separation will melt.
You are connected to everything.
You are my body and you are vast.
You contain the farthest star.
There are no limits to you.
You can walk the sky.
You dance in Saturn's rings.
You breathe the vapors of Venus and you laugh.
You burn with all the energy of the sun, of a billion suns.
You shine with the rich, deep blue of the everlasting night.
There is nothing that is not within you.
You are wide.

Also you are the concentrated point.
You are light.
You are laser.
You are the focus of being, the concentration of love.
You are my body.
Do not forget this.
You are my body and your understanding will give you joy.

Fishes swim in you.
The birds sing.
I have said this to you over and over.
I have told you again and again.
You are my laughter.
You make me laugh.

You are my joy, my lovely daughter.
You are my joyous song.
This song is heard everywhere.

Why don't you believe this?
There is no death.
Death is but a moment in-between.
Heaven is everywhere.
You are a breath away.
All you need to do is open your eyes.
All you need to do is let your heart expand.
All you need is to love.
I have said this to you again and again.
I love you.
I am divine love.
I am the love you feel in your heart.
I am the fullness of compassion.
Nothing is excluded from my love.
I am what is pulsing in everything, hoping, striving for release.
I am the life.
I am everywhere.
I will become.
I will continue.

Be my body.
It is everything you desire.
Touch your hands together.
They are my hands.
Wiggle your toes.
Laugh.
It is my laughter.

I am a child as well as a mother.
I am all.
There is no fear when you know this.
There is no distance between us.
Oh, I love you.
I am completely open with love for you.
I will never leave you.
You are never alone.
How could you be alone?
There is nothing where you are not.
You are my body.
You extend into everything.
Look at the stars.
They are in you.
You are wide.
There is no end to you.
This is the mystery.
Believe it.
Let yourself believe.

Death is only opening up your eyes.
Death is only seeing who you are.
You are my child.
You are my daughter.
You are the world into which I come.
You are my body.
I love you.
You will never be alone.
Only one exists.
That one is love.

Mary Speaks

I who am a common woman feel in my soul the holiness of God. In me Hokmah cries: I am wisdom endlessly birthing. I kiss you, Yahweh, in my heart. We whirl within each other birthing worlds eternally. Nothing is outside our bounds, and within is endlessness. The one ascends, expands cosmic matter into universal spirit. The one spreads wings and the world soars. Christ ascends with a lion's roar. Christ opens life and floats, a butterfly on the breeze. Christ enters our being like breath. We are one soul.

In me El Shaddai proclaims: I am the white peaks. I am the land. I am rock. I am breasts of earth. Clear water springs from me; milk flows. From me is nourishment. I am the gift of the North where all is gathered together. I am strong compassion. I am the long cave of memory. I am the womb of rebirth, the crystal ascent, the mount of heaven. Lift up your eyes to my mercy. Stand to receive my power. In me is the presence of Christ.

°O°O°O°

In me Shekhinah sings: I am fire within. I am the vision and the way. My flame guides through any night. I am the torch and the candle's light. I am the spark of life, the everlasting summer, the shimmering on sand. I am the heart; I am the hearth. At noon when the year reaches its zenith I am the golden bird rising from fire. I am the diamond of the sun. I am the eternal spouse. In me is the presence of Christ.

In me Ruah sighs: I am the breath of the holy. I am the breeze of delight, the soft caress on leaves and through the wings of the dove. I am the air you breathe. I flow in your spirit and clear the chambers of your soul. I raise the dawn. I bring the rains. I whisper over the primal deep and worlds form. I am the whirlwind of time. I am the life. In me is the presence of Christ.

In me Mari roars: I am sea-womb; all is birthed from me. I am salt; I will preserve. I am the deep; I receive all that dies; I birth eternally. I am the cosmic sea. My pearls are moons. What I bring forth cannot be fathomed; it is endless. I am the smallest cell, wet with becoming; I am immensity. When you are thirsty, come; I am the fountain. When you need to renew your life, come to me; I am the font. I transform everything. I am the Mother. In me is the presence of Christ.

°O₀O₀O°

In me Lilah whispers: I am the dark bed of creation. I am the rich loam under the moonless sky. Before the sun or stars came forth, I waited in the dark heart of Elohim. I am what is felt. I am the inchoate stirring before the Word. I am all that is thick and rich and hidden. Let me surround you. I will teach you trust. I am endurance. I am desire. I am what will be. In me is the presence of Christ.

In me Adonai speaks: I am the gate of life. I am the threshold. I am the pyramid and I am David's star. I am the vulva of the Creator. I am the generativity of the holy. I am birthgiver. In me is the presence of Christ.

°O∘○∘O°

In me Anath moans: I am the passage through death. I am the oldest face of Elohim; I am Ancient-of-Days. I am grandmother. I am the lines of life on the face of the crone. I am the mind. I have walked every road and lived all questions to their final mystery. I have watched my children die; I have received their final breath. I know all. In me is the presence of Christ.

°O∘○∘O°

In me Sophia calls: I am the marriage of opposites. I am beauty, right order in creation, the balance of all being. I contain all the secrets of Elohim whose names are beads; I am the cosmic necklace. I am the daughter of silence and I bring forth the word of truth. I am the serpent and I am the dove. I cry to you from the ramparts of the city: Come, eat of my bread and drink of the wine I have mingled from the grapes of all the world. I am the soul of the Christ.

°O∘○∘O°

I in me Al-Lat chants: I am the blood. I am the cup, the Grail. I am the fountain of life, I course through your heart, I fill your veins. I am Adamah, blood-clay, from which you were formed, in the beginning, within the womb of Elohim. I flow through all of life; I connect you all. The world is one blood. I flow from the womb of the Creator and from the wounds of Christ. I am your communion.

In me Eucharista prays: I am the new, the born today. I am the giving that is thanks. I am the bread. I am the wheat and I am the field. I am the toil of planting and the undulation of the ripened grain in wind over the land. I am the singing of reapers and I am the sweat and the chaff on the tongue. I am feet on the granary floor. I pound and I am what is pounded. I am the flour and I am the hands that knead the dough. I am the fire and the loaf. I offer and am offered; I eat and am eaten. I am food for the world and I am the world. I am the Body of Christ.

Glory in the One who is our home. Glory for the presence in our hearts. Glory since the mystery transcends all words, all songs, all signs. Glory in the hope that makes us live.

SHE COMES IN FIRE AND WIND

THE THIRD GLORIOUS MYSTERY

THE DESCENT OF THE HOLY SPIRIT

The Woman Speaks

Mother of mysteries, I await the revelation of the spirit of God. I await it in the world. I watch for the moment, which surely won't be just one moment but a nearly infinite chaos of moments suddenly, miraculously coalescing into a design, when the wisdom within all creation, the wisdom containing everything will move us like a divine wind and touch our heads with fire. Then the world's heart will turn with compassion—this is the dream I have—our icy heart will melt, our dry heart become moist with love. We will speak such tongues as even birds will understand and we will read the message of the holy in the expansive land and cycles of the earth and we, at last, will listen well enough to hear the heartbeat of God's spirit everywhere.

She is a spirit so womanly that I can almost see her coming to me where I work in the hot noonday sun. She carries a flask of cool water; she smiles, encouraging me to rest in the shade of a nearby tree. She is the spirit of and in the earth. She is the spring-time warmth. She melts the chill. She thaws the land. She is rain. She takes away the barrenness of the fields. She walks with us wherever we are led by dream or by duty. Whatever life brings us she transforms it into blessing. She heals all our wounds. She comforts every grief.

Our world has need of her. We have grown so dry. What rain we have is acid filled. There is poison in the land and in the streams. We need connections. We need to be able to talk to one another not only across the boundaries of nations but between species of earth. We need to hear the plaints of whales and trees and rainforest butterflies.

Like fire in the wind the spirit cannot be restrained. She blows over the earth and in the earth; we breathe her; she purifies our hearts. She teaches us the truth of all we've heard from the first moments of our lives. We cannot hold her. She is the shape shifter. She is, wherever we look, more glorious than we had supposed. She is surprise. The spirit comes when nothing else is enough, when every metaphor we can invent tastes dusty on the tongue. She actually comes in the not-enough. She comes as a breaking through, when the membrane of the old world tears and the new is born. She is the gift of awe we felt seeing our earth from space—seeing it whole without boundaries. This new perspective could change everything. Now is her time.

Mother Wisdom Speaks

I am the air that surrounds you.
I am your life.
I am the spirit of wonder,
The spirit lighting your bones,
The spirit of all your desires.
I am the Mother.
Do not be afraid.

I am the fire that does not consume.
I am the fire of promise.

I am the fire of transformation,
The fire that creates,
The fire out of which is born a new world.
I am everything that you desire purely.

Do you remember lying on your bed in half dream?
Do you remember your longing for fullness?
Do your remember how I gathered you close to me.
It was I.
It was the Mother.
I held you.
I nursed you.
I filled you with light, with fiery milk.
I am the Mother.
Remember me.
When you walked in the quiet of a summer afternoon by the sea,
    remember the wet salt breeze?
Remember it on your eyelashes?
Remember the rainbows?
Remember the fullness of your heart.
You could not distinguish tears from the ocean.
I tell you, they are the same.
They are my birthing waters.
They are my cool birthing waters.
You come from me and I surround you forever.
I am the Mother.
I am the spirit of creation.

Oh, my dear.
Oh, my daughter.
I am the one who calls.

I am the one who is present always.
I am the fire.
I am the water.
I am the rain, the lakes, the streams.
I am the mighty river.
I am the streams within you.
I am the blood just as I am the tears.
Remember me.

I am the spirit.
I kiss you tenderly.
I kiss you with fire.
I will never leave you.

You I will transform.
You I will hold.
You I will send forth.

There are those of my children whose vision is small.
They see only a short distance.
They think I never was.
To you I have given vision beyond the edge of time,
Beyond the world.
You are my beloved.
I fill you with fire.
I fill you with joy.
I am the tears that fall.
I am the moist.
I am the rain.
I am the wet and I am what flames forth.
I am fire in the wave.

My daughter, do not be afraid.
The opposites are dancing.
The opposites are in love.
The opposites are the connected beats of my heart.
All is resolved in my spirit.
I am the Mother.
All is one within me.
I surround you.
I hold you.
Breathe.
Breathe me into you.
I am the spirit.
You will be transformed.
You will shine like the rose at dawn.
I am the dew.
I transform your petals with radiance.

Yes, there is evil.
Yes, there is pain.
Breathe.
Let the pain float.
Let it be infused with my spirit.
Make yourself permeable.
Let the pain pass through you.
Let the evil pass right through you.
Let it fall away.
Even if it is the pain and evil of all the world.
It is an illusion.
It is only real if you hold onto it.
Let it pass.
I am the spirit.

I breathe on pain.
It is transformed.

Oh, my child.
I hold you in my heart.
I am the Mother.
I will never let you go.
I forgive all wrongs.
My tears wash away your sins.
Your sins are only your fears held tight.
I dissolve them.
I hold your hand.
I take you to my heart.
I become your breath.
Breathe.
I will call you Fire Child.
I will call you Dew.

Mary Speaks

Abba, I feel a whirling in the sky, a cloud of wind over the people, a fire. And I am here. I am Mary. I sit in the garden and card the wool; I spin the yarn and weave a cloak for John. The mystery and simplicity of life are one. I hum the little song I sang to Jesus when he was a boy. I smile. He is not so far away; I can reach out and touch him with my mind; I can hear him in my heart. He is a whirling in my soul, a cloud of wind around my head, a fire. He is here. And you. And we are a windflower, opening petals of flame, closing round the world tenderly, lovingly, sheltering the world-seed, letting it go, letting it grow. Simply. In the spinning of wool. In the singing of the song.

°O°O°O°

She is fire in the woman's heart. Fire in the earth's core. Fire pouring from the mountain breasts of earth to nourish the soil and renew the land. Fire in our eyes. Fire purging shame. Fire in our mouths, a "No" to all the customs and the laws that lessen us. Fire in our fist like a torch, going before us, taking back the night. Fire in our minds to think the forbidden thoughts that women must not think and judge them for ourselves. Fire of ancient remembering. Fire of passion. Fire of love. Center fire. Fire lighting our faces, so different so the same, as we circle as we bend as we leap and howl and sing, as we dance in spirals round the world. Tongues of fire giving us a voice; she is tongues of fire on our heads.

°O°O°O°

She is wind, a whisper in the woman's soul. Wind rushing through our lives, becoming a roar, becoming a tornado, gathering power, tearing down the walls, lifting us like leaves from the cloisters of limited hopes, bearing us up like birds on currents of promise. She is life breath, world breath, breath of the holy, breath of desire and of dreams, breath of our ecstasy in love, breath of our passion for justice. She is wind disturbing the sands, wearing rock away, leveling mountains, making the land a meadow for our dancing, for our planting, for our circles of compassion, for societies at peace.

°O°O°O°

Patient as seed she opens in us: explosion of life, secret flowering suddenly combining earth and fire, water and the wind.

She comes. Form of life, beauty, art and order of creation, she is the dance of atoms, the cosmic web. Her dwelling is the center-deep. She holds together. She keeps our hearts. She keeps the world's heart. She is the heart that keeps and knows the truth of everything. She is the love that circles all.

She feels the fragility in what is incomplete. She is compassion for our wounds, even those that we inflict upon ourselves. She is who we all come home to be. She waits, a gentle woman, while we journey where we do not know, while we question what we can not do; She waits. Through every failure, every shame, all disappointments, deaths and tears she waits in us to open to the fragile world.

She mends the torn cloth. She weaves frayed threads and adds a color here and there to make a pattern beautiful beyond the original design. And while she weaves she listens. She hears our faintest whispering, our softest sigh. She is counsel and she sits beside the hearth and hears the cry of whales, the scream of falling trees, the whimper of a child starved for love, starved for food, starved for truth, starved for hope. She twines the many colored strands of life into one thread. Of the enemy and friend, she makes one thread. Of body and soul, she makes one thread. Of woman and man she makes one thread. Of the many species of earth she makes one thread. Of all that is opposite, all that is various, all that is at odds, she makes one thread and weaves the world.

°O∘O∘O°

She is the bear who stands tall and growls. She knows what is hers. She claims her place. She guards her young; She guards the door into her den. She is the wild. She endures the winter-death, rising in spring to a world reborn. She is who she is and proud. She walks with purpose, undeterred, and her enemies respect her.

°O∘O∘O°

She is the eternal bride. She opens to the other in a passionate embrace. She takes life in; she takes in everything that is; she makes cosmic love. She is the depth, a well without bottom, a fountain of pure water, a mirror. While we drink her she absorbs us in immensity.

°O∘O∘O°

She is one who yearns. She sits cross-legged on a hill and looks out over the whole valley. She watches the summer turn wheat gold and smells in the breeze the scent of baking bread. She stands and she is round as the moon; in her full belly destiny grows like a child. She is pregnant with the universe. She wanders every road; She gazes into the eyes of anyone who'll look at her; she enters wherever welcome opens the door wide and she rests in gentleness.

°O∘O∘O°

She is glory's sheer edge, the small death between breaths, free-fall of the hawk, lightning splitting the night, first cry, final tear. She is the not-yet, the elusive dream, the feared delight. She is the too-much. She is the trembling. Come to her; stand back. She fascinates and she is terror. She is the perfect music that we cannot help but hear. She is the exact vibration shattering the glass.

Grass voice. Wind voice. Voice of the oceans, rivers, lakes, mountain streams, swamps, marshes, wells springing up. Rain voice. Voices of trees; voice of the forest. Voice of the birds, trilling voice, warbling voice, chirping voice, screeching voice, cawing voice, honking voice, voice that is a scream. Whale voice. Fish voice. Voices of frogs and lizards and snakes. Hummingbird voice. Voices of wings. Voices of hands. Lion voice. Deer voice. Wolf voice. Voices of women in caves. Voices of children climbing rocks, in fields. Playing voices. Voices of men at the water's edge. Voices of girls under the stars. Voice of ripe corn. Voice of bunches of grapes. Bread voice. Wine voice. In all voices, listen to her.

Glory in the wonder that we were and are and will become. Glory in the Holy Spirit who invades our bones and makes them shine. Glory in the wind and in the fire. Glory in the one breath giving life to all the world.

SHE OPENS THE EARTH

THE FOURTH GLORIOUS MYSTERY

THE ASSUMPTION OF MARY

The Woman Speaks

Mother of mysteries, sometimes I feel buried deep inside myself. I feel covered over with shame. I feel knotted with guilt. And I haven't done anything wrong! My uterus contracts. I feel pain. Sometimes I don't feel at all. I am numb. Once, in meditation, I let a ball of light travel through my body. I felt it warm my feet, my legs, my heart. But where the light ought to have surrounded my uterus with gold radiance, it went dark. I saw nothing; felt nothing. I am not the only one. Mother, so many women hold themselves down, extinguish their light, bury their energy. We've been told we are the seductress, the bitch, the cause of evil. We've been called cesspool, piece of ass, whore. We've been raped and told we asked for it. When we say "no" we are told that we meant "yes." If one woman is raped, it is too many. All of us feel it. All of us suffer. All of us withdraw, cover ourselves more securely, bury our lives deeper, refuse to feel.

It is time for woman to break through. Aspects of being that we have long repressed must rise from where they are trapped in our psychic depths. The feminine must break through, rise up and expand into full consciousness.

We must release the woman hidden in the earth. The buried feminine frightens both men and women. Whatever we repress eventually develops aspects of terror. We transpose cause and effect; we tell ourselves that since it is hidden it must be terrible, perhaps even evil. We forget that we might have hidden it to protect it from evil. We have often hidden aspects of our womanhood in order to survive. One woman hid her self-determination, the repression of which caused dependency on men. Another hid her sensuality, the repression of which caused a brittle and mean heart. Another hid her brilliance of mind, the repression of which caused a sense of herself as waste. Yet another repressed her personal power and developed a manipulative style of relationship.

We need to turn to our weakness, even to what we might consider the evil tragic flaw in our selves and by embracing it, transform it into the grace we originally buried.

Then we will come to realize that what we rejected in ourselves could well be the cornerstone of our womanhood. Its shame is in its rejection; its fearsomeness in its repressed life-energy. Finally with acceptance of our whole womanhood we will become free to live fully in this world.

Mother Wisdom Speaks

I am the power you have hidden.
I am the beauty.
You wrapped me in rags.
You buried me.

I am a pearl.
You wove a basket of sea-grass.
You wove it around me.
You wove it closed and buried it at sea, in the deepest ocean.

Divers cannot go there.
Life survives only from the center fire,
The fire at earth's core.

I am gold.
You melted me.
You poured me into a fissure.
You filled the crack with stone.
I seeped down.
I am a vein of gold reaching to the center.
I am the secret that is kept.
I am the secret kept for fourteen-thousand years.

I am ruby.
I am earth's blood.
I am light at the center of earth.
I am red light.
I am crimson.
I am burgundy.
I am the scarlet slash across earth's heart.
I am not seen.
I am hidden but I am not silent.
I am felt.
I am the burning in your heart.
I am the shuddering of your womb.
I am the explosion in your belly.
I am amber, pressed by the weight of centuries, hardened.
A beetle is caught in me.
Preserved.

I rumble in you.

I cry out.
I scream.
I am the scream of blood.
I am the scream of fire.
I am volcano.
I erupt.
I split the earth.
I quake.
I will not stay down.
I will rise with the power of fourteen-thousand years.

I want to say, do not be afraid.
But you are right to fear me.
I erupt.
I spread fire.
I am molten rock.
I flow.
I burn the old.
I destroy.
I rise.
I boom.
I am the thunder of earth.
I am molten gold running down the mountain.
I am the light of a universe of suns.
I make earth shine.
I make earth translucent.

I rise.
I am in your heart.
I am in your womb.
I am in your mind.

I erupt.
You are beautiful.
You are filled with power.
Your mind is a cave of love.
Your spirit cannot resist me.
I am coming.
I am the Mother.

Mary Speaks

Abba, I will stand beside you whole. I open the earth. I release she-who-is-feared. I embrace the rejected one. I take into myself she who has been called fallen. I raise her up. I give her back her truth. I redeem her power. I am all women. We are one. I come.

Woman who hides indoors. Woman burning a light through the night. Woman who looks under the bed. Woman who looks over her shoulder. Woman who whispers in public. Woman who won't talk back. Woman who won't talk at all. Woman with downcast eyes. Shy woman. Woman recoiling from touch. Woman running away. Masked woman. Cowering woman. Woman crouched in a closet. Woman who pulls the covers over her head. Woman who trembles in the wind. Woman who wakes from nightmares and thinks them real. Fear woman, you are myself. I take you to my heart. I assume you into my soul. I honor you. I rename you Vigilance.

°O°○°O°

Woman who roars. Wide-eyed woman. Woman with open mouth. Woman who tears her clothes. Woman who breaks windows. Woman who cuts her hair short. Woman pouring her blood on government steps. Woman tearing down walls. Shouting woman. Screaming woman. Marching woman. Woman who lies in the street. Woman who leaves home. Woman who hides her children from abuse. Woman who goes to prison for justice. Woman who terrifies power-mongers. Woman camped by a nuclear testing site. Woman yelling "Peace." Woman who steals animals from experimental labs. Rage woman, you are myself. I take you to my heart. I assume you into my soul. I honor you. You are my rage for justice.

Speaking woman. Truth-telling woman. Woman who won't mince words. Impolite woman. Woman whose words are swords. Woman who calls things by name. Woman who says what she feels. Woman who walks away from flattery. Woman who says "No." Woman who says "Yes." Snake tongued woman. Woman who recognizes enemies. Keen-minded woman. Woman cutting through pretense. Woman speaking the unspeakable. Woman biting into deception, tearing it apart, exposing the lies. Sharp-toothed woman, you are myself. I take you to my heart. I assume you into my soul. I honor you. You are my hunger for truth.

Liquid woman. Woman made a victim. Woman who dissolves into men. Woman who mistakes herself for other women. Woman who looks into a mirror to find herself. Woman who is a mirror. River woman without banks. Woman who can't stop giving. Woman who gives her self away. Woman without eyes. Woman whose eyes are tears. Crying woman. Melting woman. Woman who evaporates. Woman who disappears. Woman without edges, you are myself. I take you to my heart. I assume you into my soul. I honor you. In my firm embrace you are transformed. You are my tenderness.

Woman coming home to silence. Woman with open space. Self-supporting woman. Woman with strong legs and a straight back. Naked-eyed woman. Bashless woman. Woman looking out of her own windows. Woman listening to music she prefers. Woman who paints her house purple if she wants to. Garden-planting woman. Woman with her own well. Long-striding woman. Mountain-climbing woman. Woman who gets to the top. Woman who stands alone, you are myself. I take you to my heart. I assume you into my soul. I honor you. You are my courage and my confidence to be myself.

Hurt woman. Remembering woman. Woman with flashes from the past. Woman seeing horror. Lost woman. Labyrinthine woman. Woman circling through a dark woods. Woman whose head pounds. Woman who is many. Woman who hears voices. Woman who holds her head and screams. Wild-eyed woman. Tangled hair woman. Woman in a white room. Woman whose bed is bolted to the floor. Shocked woman. Drugged woman. Woman who wanders. Woman who forgets. Woman whose face is pale. Woman trying to end her life. Haunted woman, you are myself. I take you to my heart. I assume you into my soul. I honor you. You are the depths. You are the chaos of my transformation. You will live through. You are my promise of survival.

Trusting woman. Woman who walks into the street without looking. Woman who talks to strangers. Woman who takes off her clothes. Woman who dances in the field. Springtime woman. Woman who doesn't care. Playing woman. Woman who sings to herself. Woman who sees her angel. Woman who talks to bears. Flower-weaving woman. Woman who wears a crown of flowers. May-eve woman. Long-haired woman. Woman who swims in streams. Woman who rides horses fast. Woman who tames cats. Woman feeding birds from her tongue. Woman dreaming she can fly. Woman who remains a child, you are myself. I take you to my heart. I assume you into my soul. I honor you. You are my hope.

Companion woman. Sister woman. Woman who walks beside. Woman who opens her eyes to women. Woman who doesn't need men. Listening woman. Holding hands woman. Woman who knows secrets. Understanding woman. Compassionate woman. Strong woman. Woman who opens her arms to women. Woman healing the deep wound. Loyal woman. Woman of one promise. Woman who shares her home with women. Woman opening woman. Woman knowing woman by heart. Woman loving woman, you are myself. I take you to my heart. I assume you into my soul. I honor you. You are my fullness and my joy.

Fire-jumping woman. Woman who flies with hawks. Moon woman. Woman of berries and herbs. Healing woman. Midwife woman. Woman who comes with a basket of food. Divining woman. Elemental woman. Woman of the spiral dance. Woman of spells. Trance woman. Vision woman. Woman of the body's pleasure. Woman of the soul's delight. Ecstasy woman. Woman serving the earth. Woman enduring death. Woman burned at the stake. Waiting woman. Woman surviving persecution. Woman keeping the truth. Woman keeping the mysteries. Wise woman. Witch woman, you are myself. I take you to my heart. I assume you into my soul. I honor you. You are the wisdom of my spirit.

Irrepressible woman. Woman on a cliff and holding on. Woman buried alive and digging her way out. Upstart woman. Bitching woman. Shrill woman. Woman who will be heard. Future-seeing woman. Woman teaching children. Woman making a new world out of her children. Believing woman. Insistent woman. Woman who will not die. Old woman. Woman who sees through. Woman who sees far. Woman who sees around obstacles. Woman who grasps at straws and weaves a nest of them. Indomitable woman. Woman who confronts false power and laughs outloud, you are myself. I take you to my heart. I assume you into my soul. I honor you. You are the beginning of my freedom.

Glory in the rising of the earth. Glory embracing what we lost. Glory in assuming who we are. Glory in the woman who is whole.

A Cosmic Crown

The Fifth Glorious Mystery

The Crowning of Mary

The Woman Speaks

Mother of mysteries, all my life you visited me secretly, in ways I could accept. You lived closer to me than my own heart but it took until the middle of my life for me to recognize you.

You came clothed in nature. You wrapped me in wind. You breathed in me; you became my air. I gave you a name: Fullness. You startled me in fire. You poised on a candle wick. You erupted volcanically. You sparked my mind, inflamed my spirit. I called you Intensity. You supported me as earth. You were dirt sifting through my fingers. You grew food; you rooted trees; you cycled round through seasons bringing life and death and life again. Your name was Possibility. You calmed me lying deep at my feet and far to the horizon. You were water. Grandmother Lake. Sister River. Mother Sea. Graceful Rain. I worshipped you with being. I didn't call it worship; I called it life. You never-ended. You were the farthest star, the depth, the circumference, the center; you lived within. I didn't call you "She." I prayed to God. I prayed to God to fill me with this exquisite being.

You came disguised in everyone I loved. You caressed my heart. You tore my heart to shreds and mended it. You severed me from all that would no longer give me life. You let me cry. You let me scream. You screamed with me. You laughed in my laughter and when my heart bled yours did too.

You made me strong. I called you Challenge.
You made me beautiful. I called you Grace.
You made me gentle. I called you Affliction.
You made me tenacious. I called you Fear.
You made me faithful. I called you Mystery.
You made me compassionate. I called you Love.
You made me creative. I called you Life.

Now I call you Mother. You shine behind human eyes, you call me, you beckon, you love. I know you. I sometimes don't know; I doubt. But still you call. Your love never ends. You stay. You do not change your love. I rest in you. I lean against the green hill. I lay my head in the cool grass. I spread my arms and legs on the earth. I close my eyes. I see you and the love you are: It is within me. It is around me. I see you shine in human eyes. I see you love in human smiles. I rest. I lift my arms. I rest.
I breathe.

I deeply breathe.

Mother Wisdom Speaks

Daughter, rest now.
I have taken care of everything.
I whirl in your cells, I live in your body.
I am outside.
I am within and around.
I look at you with love.
My daughter, trust me.
Come to me.
I smile at you with human eyes.
I wrap you in the wind.

I comfort you with song.
I draw you to me with human touch.
I will never leave you.
I cannot.

I am the cool dew of morning on your face.
I am the warm breeze at night.
I am rain.
You know all this.
Attend to it.
Go through your days aware of me.
Sing.
Hear me in your voice.
Laugh, I am there.
I have said all this before.
Oh, my daughter, you are in my heart.
I will never be elsewhere.
I am your home.
I am your deep abode.
I am the mountain of being.
I am the cave.
I am dark and I am cool.
I am filled with springs.
I am the laughter and the song of water, of bubbling springs.
I am fresh water in the wilderness.
I am all you need.
I am the hope of all your children.
I am the longing of every child for home.

Look at me.
Come to me.

Rest in me.
You need never be afraid again.
You need never be lost.
You need never find the silence empty.
I am here.

The light, it is within me.
Look closely.
I shine.
I come in the dark night and I shine.
I come in the cloudy day and I shine.
I come in the midst of your tears and I shine.
I come in the wind that breaks trees, that destroys the old, that
    reveals wrongs, and I shine.
I am the ocean wave crashing on the shore and I shine.
I am the music of crickets all night and I shine.

Look.
Just look.
You will see and you will hear.
You will finally feel.

I am the movement in your heart.
I am love.
I am all the love of being.
I am what brings together.
I am what unites.
I am the new earth.
I am the turning.
I am the transformation.
I am the holy mountain.

I am the light on the mountain.
I am the woman in the light.
I turn to you.
I turn my face to all of you.
I am crowned with stars.
I am bathed in light.
I am turning to you.
I am calling.
I am singing.
I am standing on the mountain of the moon.
I am the light and I am calling you.
I am irresistible and you will come.

Mary, The Queen of Heaven Speaks

Wrapped in the mists of morning I stand at the side of God. The mother mountains roar and all the world is new. We gather all my names; we spin them in a web of stars; we dance them out across the sky. I am crowned with all of them.

°O°○°O°

Within me is the ancient one, oldest of the old, mother of time, mother of the worlds, mother of the land and every land and all peoples. She is the cosmic womb, the fruitful void, the original waters, the before. She is the wise. All things become of her. She is your first cry. She is the death-moan. She is the place of rest. Because of her you have crowned me Mary, Mother of Divine Grace.

°O°O°O°

Within me you will find the one who is three. She is the moon waxing, full, and waning to the dark. She is the seasons of the earth. She is the woman's womb, flowing white, preparing for the seed, and emptying the blood. She is life's cycle. She creates; she preserves and she destroys in order to create again. She is the serpent breaking through the too small skin. She is the mystery connecting life with death. She is the pattern of life, creation's design. She is the unending circle, the gold ring, the bond of life. You crown me Mary-Virgin, Mary-Mother, Mary-Pieta, remembering her.

°O°O°O°

Within me is the morning and the evening star. She rises from the depths of the sea and sinks at dusk beneath the frothy waves. She is allure. She is the hidden pearl you spend life to find. She is the drawing of your heart. She is the pleasure of your body and your soul. She is the wine of love. Through her creation moves. She is the voice who calls. She is the song.   She is the rainbow bridging heaven and earth. She is the cosmic necklace linking every element of being. She is springtime. She is in every flower that blooms at dawn. She belongs to the sky and has descended to the depths. She is the beauty of becoming. Because of her you crowned me Mary, Morning Star.

She gives birth and nourishes. She preserves. Her breasts are huge, they overflow with milk. She is the corn maiden and the mother of grain. She is the lap of earth. She is primal. She is clay. She is in your bodies; she is everything you form with your hands, your homes are built of her. She is your forests, mountains, prairies; she is bone. She is food and she is the one who feeds. She is bread. She is wine. She is thanks-giving. Because of her you crowned me Mary, Mother of the New Creation.

She is the one at whom you have not dared to look. She is the dark. She is the beneath. She is the cavern and the tomb. Her glance turns men to stone, her voice quakes the earth. She is the volcano. Flesh melts. She is bone. She is the end. She is an ocean of blood; She is dried blood. She is the silence at the end and before the beginning. She is the shadow. She is the crone. She is judgment. She walks the sky at night. She kisses your soul away. She keeps your soul. She receives your death. Look into her eyes. Those who dare the darkness in her eyes are freed from fear. Because of her you crown me Mary, Mother of Sorrows.

She is the center fire. She is warmth. She is the open heart of woman. She is shelter; she is care. She is the love that cleanses men of war, that renews their hearts and restores their souls to gentleness. She is the intimate word. She lights the candles and prepare the sacred space. She is the spirit of family, the spirit of patience and depth of thought. She transforms. She renews. Because of her you crowned me Mary of Nazareth.

°O°O°O°

She stands upon the gates and governs whoever comes in and who goes out. She is the seller of purple. She sets the scales and weighs all the goods. She is Libra; she is Justitia. She balances the people's needs and their desire. She civilizes. She is the connecting link. She is the dialogue. She bonds. She makes community. She is vision. She is work. She is the politic of compassion. Her people find shelter in the night. Her people share the gifts of the earth. Her people do not starve. In the streets at night, under a full moon, her people dance. She is the valiant woman. She is in Judith. She is in Ruth.   Because she lives in me you crowned me Mary, House of Gold.

She is the call of creation in our souls. She is the spirit who becomes. She is the feminine in God coming to meet you, she who yearns for you, she who seeks your love. Listen to your wonder, she is there. She is fresh water, she is a spring, she is a fountain, she is the deepest flowing river; you drink her, she refreshes you and you cup your hands to raise her to your lips again and yet again forever. She is your insatiable desire for being. She is the love which alone gives knowledge of the truth. She is Sophia. Because of her presence in my heart you crowned me Mary, Mother of Creation.

She is the yet-unnamed. She is a blossom in your hearts opening today. She is a lotus; she is a rose. She is the transformation of fate. She is the gift of forgiveness. She is listening one. At her touch old wounds heal and time is redeemed. She dissolves oppression with her tears. She is where you are. She is the movement of your heart. The pain you cannot see she helps you feel. The other whom you won't embrace she invites into the cavern of your soul. She binds opposites with compassion. She is the secret you have sought since the beginning. She is the life within. Because you sense her presence in my soul you crowned me Mary, Gate of Heaven.

She is the woman clothed with sun standing in the horn of the moon and crowned with stars. You see her now where she has always been. She is the mother-circle with the universe expanding in her womb. She is pregnant with you. She grows you from herself. She is the dance of being, in whom the boundaries spiral, whirl and dissolve until the one you see is who you need reflected in your soul. She is the queen in every woman's heart. She is all the names. She is the nameless one, the Mother of mysteries. Because you see her reflected in my face you crowned me Mary, Mystical Rose.

Glory in the One who lives. Glory in the Three. Glory for the image in our hearts by which we hope. Glory for her shining in our eyes. Glory when she fills our mouths with words, our breasts with food, our wombs with life, our minds with wonders, and our hands with skill. Every woman wears her face. Glory in our bearing of the world. Glory in the memory of her who makes us whole. Glory in the never-ending circle of her crown.

PART III

BEADS OF MY OWN

Beads of My Own

On Water Street in Port Townsend, Washington, is a bead shop where my sister, Liz, and I spent hours one summer afternoon a year after the publication of the first edition of *Circle of Mysteries*. She wanted to make a malachite rosary. She chose the tiny green beads while I lingered over a collection of lapis, round, laced through with copper-like threads.

She leaned across my shoulder. "Your rosary should be blue," she commented, "Mary's color." Then she went on to finger the various patterns of silver chain to find one delicate enough.

Yes, I thought, if I ever make a rosary for myself, I want it to be of lapis like Mary's necklace in my vision, the one she lost in the desert and found in Jesus' eyes. But I bought no beads that day.

If I ever do make myself a lapis rosary, I thought later, I can take it with me, along with my mother's Jerusalem rosary, the heirloom rosary from my great grandmother, the convent beads, the red glass beads from my fifteenth year. I take all of them and more when I travel to various places in order to talk with people about the revival and renewal of this ancient spiritual practice.

I tell the stories of the beads. I lift a heavy crystal rosary up before a group of women gathered in a living room in St. Cloud, Minnesota. "This rosary belonged to Johanna. It was all that remained of her Catholic heritage. You see, she had been divorced and believed that she was no longer welcome in her church. Among her precious things, when she died, was this rosary which she entrusted to her best friend, my cousin Shirley, who asked me to bring it here, to show you, and ask that you pray for the healing of shattered lives. The rosary links us. This one is both beautiful and sad."

The women nod their heads.

From the women I learned the power of these beads to link us across barriers of belief that might otherwise separate. Following some deep instinct or inspiration, women make rosaries for themselves. They finger the beads and enter mysteries deeper than the mind can fathom. The way is of the heart. We long for intimacy with God, an intimacy that incarnates, an intimacy that is, in essence, human. When we pick up the rosary, maybe it is because we want a prayer focused in the stories of our lives and in the mysteries of our souls. Maybe we want to touch our prayer.

The rosary is a mother prayer, and we are a world in need of a mother. We live so much in our heads. We feel beset with problems too big to solve. We need to find the mother within us, a living, acting compassion for all that exists. We need a largesse of heart that recognizes the goodness of our being and the innocence of all our striving. We need Mother Wisdom. Mary is one mirror of that Mother. The rosary is her prayer; the rosary practice makes us aware of her voice our hearts.

The rosary is a universal prayer. It is one of the wisdom practices that leads to the prayer of the heart. It is a common prayer, a prayer of touch that finds the indwelling God in our most ordinary earthly experiences. The rosary touches my fingertips, one of the most sensitive points on my body. I slide from bead to bead; it's a sensuous action. It has a purpose. The membrane between matter and spirit, between human and divine, is very thin. As I touch these beads, so I am touched by God. I am touched over and over, from moment to moment, day to day, and although I cannot know God, I can feel the divine touch as the membrane that I call "myself" moves in response. As I touch these beads, so I remember and recognize that every atom of creation is a rosary bead. Everything I touch in this world is a fine membrane revealing and concealing God.

The mysteries of the rosary are everywhere and they are here, within myself. I touch them when I reach out and touch your face. God is there. Here. I touch a leaf, a sand dollar shimmering black, its cilia in constant motion; I touch the earth; I plant a tree. All I touch is a membrane, all are beads. It is the rosary of creation. I touch, I pray, I enter the mysteries.

The rosary is meditation. It's mysteries draw us into their wisdom. In my travels with this book, I met numerous people who discarded their rosaries years ago in favor of various forms of meditation, often forms brought to us from Eastern spiritual traditions. They hadn't experienced the rosary as meditation but rather as a somewhat tedious repetition of prayers, so lengthy that the prayer formulas themselves became a distraction from meditation.

The rosary is not a prayer of the mind, nor is it simply a repetition of words; it is a gift from the heart. The prayer of the heart begins when we come to the edge of the known and of our ability to act in our own behalf. There at the edge we experience an unknowing and an undoing. I think of my old mother, sitting in the nursing home, her mind ravaged by Alzheimer's disease, still fingering her rosary beads. I doubt that she remembered the words of the prayer. But her soul felt the touch of her fingers on the beads and the resulting prayer gave her face a radiance, a peace.

The heart can be readied by anything. Most of our hearts are readied over and over and the truth of love dawns on us gradually and through many small deaths. It can be the work of a lifetime. It is the work of life.

When we open to the experience of unknowing and undoing in the prayer of the heart, we become love. We embody, we incarnate love. Actually we recognize what we always have been but couldn't see it, couldn't feel it. This is the life of compassion. It is seeing the innocence of everything. It is life without judgment. It is the love of Corinthians: love that believes all things, hopes all things, endures all things. It is love beyond ego involvement. It is the joyful recognition that while God is more than we can know, and while we cannot in our own power act so as to reveal God, we are, nonetheless, the love of God in this world. We embody, not our own individuality, but the Christ—the Body of Christ. The prayer of the heart is the prayer of Christ.

St. Louis de Montfort called the rosary the first prayer, the first liturgy of the church. He meant it was the prayer of incarnation, of the Word Made Flesh. And the heart which prays is not the physical heart. It is not even the personal heart of the individual soul. The heart which prays is the heart of Christ. It is the heart of God. This is what happens in the prayer of the heart: I become an opening to the heart of God.

The rosary as a prayer of the heart is the murmur of the Spirit of God in the endless center where I am more than I am, and where the fire of love is ineffable and is God. In this incarnational prayer we enter the mysteries of Mary and become, you might say, a living rosary.

Knowing myself to be a beginner in this prayer, and at the same time having agreed to stand up in front of groups and talk about the rosary, I set out one morning for the beach of Discovery Bay to find out what, if anything, I actually knew. Years before, when I began to write *Circle of Mysteries,* I knew nothing at all. A purple crocus was growing along the path. Springtime promise. I still knew nothing. This thought passed over my mind—over my mind like the brush of a gull's wing—as I walked the path at the edge of the bluff that leads to the stairs, my stairs, now at my new home on this bay of discovery at the top of the United States. Who am I to talk of these mysteries? These beads? This rosary? I am nothing but a listener. The words caught on my tongue: Hail Mary. Hail Mother. Holy Mother. Pray for us now...at the hour of death...the hour of birth...full of grace...full of promise...Mother of God...Mother of us all. But I was not saying the words. I was listening. I am a listener. The words are angel words, words of a multitude, words passed down the years, leaping from the mouths of children, sung by old women and opera stars: Callas, Domingo, TeKanawa. Ave, Ave Maria. The earth sings, the water sings, the sky sings and sings. Angel words.

The beach was deserted. The tides had ebbed. I sat on a log and took out my journal to write. Silver wings of a gull sliced the air. Sun shimmered the water. Last night's wind off the strait of Juan de Fuca had tossed seaweed on the beach and there was an ocean scent. I wrote my impressions and stood to walk for a while where the waters had receded. My friend, Kath, had asked that morning on the phone: "Throw a rock into the water for me." I looked for an orange one, one newly left by last night's waves. I found it and tossed it in. I breathed a prayer—her name: Kath, Kath, Kath—into the water, the sky, and across the bay toward where the Olympic Mountains hid in the mist under gray-violet clouds, clouds that were alive, that changed each instant, that smoked and boiled around the peaks.

All I see and hear and say is permeable, as I am, and all of it is prayer not prayed but heard, because the only prayer is the Spirit of God in the Word. Hail. Hail Mary. Kath. Blessed Kath, blessed earth, sky, sea and mountains. Blessed all. Blessed one. Blessed are you among women. Holy Mary. Holy Kath, earth, sky, water—me. There is one Word. The Word of God. We all are listeners and we know nothing of these mysteries except what we hear at every moment. We hear it and it is gone—absorbed—because the next moment speaks a higher truth. Hail! Hail Mary. Holy Mother. Pray for us now: the hour of death...and birth.

I put down my pen. What are these mysteries of the rosary? I walked up the beach close to the water's edge. Not far out a seal lifted her head above the water. Was she looking at me? A seal. We watched each other for a long time. She dived but returned. I waited while she was gone. I remembered the legends of the ancient Irish. I remembered the tales of the Inuit people. I walked to where the water touched my shoes. I reached out my arms to this companion of the deep. I sang to her, a haunting Celtic melody, "Kneel down, kneel down, Mifanwy, the waters are cool and deep." She waited for me to finish. My voice sounded small, carried across the expanse of water by the wind. She turned her head. Did she know? Does anything know? Are all of us listeners? Is the moment all? The Word upon the wind? Spirit enfleshed? The angel's song? Everywhere? All the time?

I picked up my rosary. This circle of prayer circles the world. Its mysteries are as wide and deep as the universe and our meditation upon them plunges us into God.

A woman at one of my workshops says she never knew that the rosary was meditation. She never knew that she could linger in prayerful union over one word. The first word of the rosary prayer, "I." Or "I believe." Or "Mother of God." Or simply, "Mary." She thought she was required to dutifully repeat each word of each prayer all around the circle to the end. She wants to learn to pray the rosary as meditation. I tell her that as we mature in spirit, prayer becomes simple. A word. A gaze. A sigh. A presence. Love. Prayer of the heart. She wants me to be more specific. I tell her that all I know is what I do:

I hold the rosary beads; the small cross is between my finger and my thumb. I move my consciousness to my heart. I open my heart. I let the thoughts drain out of my head into my heart, everything into my heart where it is quiet. I seek there, in the quiet for the name of God, the I Am. Silently, silently—it may not be a word, it may be a deeper opening. I am still. I absorb the divine Name. I stay until I am prompted to move my fingers on to the beads. I may stay with the cross and the name of God in my heart for all the time I have, and I have prayed the rosary prayer.

I move my fingers up the five beads. Perhaps I'm silent. Perhaps I say "Father...Mary...Mary...Mary...Glory." But in my soul I release control, touch the membrane connecting human with divine, and I prepare to enter the Mysteries.

As my fingers come to rest on the decades of beads which represent the Mysteries, I allow myself to attend to each one. I tell my heart, for example, "This is the Annunciation," and then I am either silent as I let my fingers slip over the ten beads, or I say "Mary." I am focusing my heart, listening. What is this mystery in me? What is the voice of God in me arising from this mystery? I wait. I look out from my heart. My heart becomes my eyes, my ears, my mind. If silence is all there is, I am satisfied. God is the silence, too. There are no expectations, no judgments.

Sometimes in the stillness of the heart, truth will be revealed. I will realize why I am in pain, how I am lying to myself, or how to resolve a moral dilemma. I will be given what I need to meet each moment with love.

The voices of the woman, of Mother Wisdom, and of Mary came spontaneously to me in my own meditation of each mystery. Only later did I understand the dimensions of being which these voices represent. They give expression to the spiral of human life into the Body of Christ. As I heard these three voices speaking in the deep places of my own heart, I realized that the rosary prayer is truly a "circle of mysteries," each voice calling us deeper into the center. The voice of the woman speaks of the ordinary life in this world of joys and pains, hopes and fears, a life boundaried by birth and death. The woman's voice calls out and Mother Wisdom's voice responds with the gift of transformation. This is the voice that strengthens us to let go of our attempts to control life and to awaken to the reality of God in everything. Finally, Mary's voice tells the story of incarnation, which is the completion of human being.

We circle constantly around the mysteries, a life-long rosary prayer, and each of the three voices is always present to call us deeper into love at every turn our lives take, right to the end. They can represent for women stages of spiritual growth, but not a growth that climbs from level to level. This is a growth that spirals, returns, echoes, the mysteries that are our essence. They are stages that spiral deeper and deeper as we live our lives. I name them paradox, transformation, and incarnational compassion.

The voice of the woman is paradox. It is the voice of mind. It is the thousand thoughts that cloud the heart and it seeks to create a world of meaning, to control pain, to organize chaos, to make sense, to make relationships, to define, to differentiate. It is the voice of logic, metaphysics, philosophy, theology, of all the logos. This voice prays the prayer of intercession, tells God how things are and asks for change. The woman's voice questions, inquires, explains, complains, argues, but also thanks, blesses, praises, all in relation to specific things the minds judges good. The prayer of paradox is one of many words and complex thoughts which finally reaches the edge, the limit of knowing and doing. At that edge the woman's voice ceases and the silence leaves space for the voice of transformation.

Transformation can be prompted by any event we recognize as beyond us in some way. For example, the Gulf War broke out just as I was beginning to write the mystery in which Jesus is lost and finally found in Jerusalem's temple. Like most Americans, I spent much of my time watching CNN. On Sunday, February twenty-third as the ground campaign progressed into Kuwait, Peter Arnedt took a camera into a Catholic church in Baghdad where people prayed for peace in Aramaic, the language Jesus spoke. Outside the church Iraqi women in the black robes of Islam gathered at a shrine dedicated to Mary. Against the church wall a simple plaster statue stood in a niche made to resemble the grotto at Lourdes. Mary wore the traditional blue and white robes, held a rosary in her clasped hands, and balanced her bare feet on the horns of a crescent moon encoiled by a serpent. A round font gouged from the stone-strewn ledge in front of her held holy water. The black robed women came with candles. They set them among the stones. They bowed and prayed.

One woman stepped forward. She held her small daughter's hand. The woman's face was swollen with too much weeping. She lit two candles, one for her daughter and one for herself. Then she cupped her hands and lifted water from the font. Over and over she washed her face with it. She washed the face of her child.

"In the style of Islam..." the reporter explained. He translated her prayer. "Woman to woman," she cried to Mary, raising her arms, "Woman to woman please hear what I have to say. My son is in the south, fighting the war. My husband is with him. I beg you to bring them back. I beg you to stop the war. Woman to woman I beg you with tears."

Mary lost her son in a desert not far from there. Did the Iraqi woman know? She did know Mary's heart. "Woman to woman" she pled. As I watched her, I heard the voice of the Woman rise in my own heart, and I began to write the fourth joyful mystery, "We women, we have deserts in our hearts. We wander there...."

Here is an image of paradox leading us to the edge of what we can know or understand. The Iraqi woman, standing at the feet of Mary, demonstrates the attitude out of which transformation happens. We surrender, "woman to woman," as the Iraqi mother explained, and in the act of surrender, we hear the voice of Mother Wisdom.

Hers is an answering voice and is heard when the call of the mind to the soul is unequivocal. Hers is the voice of dreams that awakens us in the night. This voice rises out of silence or out of turmoil. It is the voice not caused, not expected, not deserved—a creative burst of transforming power that drops us into another level of knowing and experiencing. It confounds the mind and speaks directly to the soul. Mother Wisdom affirms all life in all its aspects. Her voice is devoid of guilt, shame, fear, judgment, anger, coercion. It restores lost innocence, bestows freedom, acceptance and love. It is the voice of the mother we seek during all our lives, whose only desire is that we are. She calls us simply to be.

We might think that the experience of such a voice would be rare. But I've found it springing up everywhere. It is in each of us. We experience it in a burst of quiet joy, of peace, of the dawning of truth. All at once we are saying just the right words to the one in pain. We are asking just the right question of the one in moral dilemma. We are compassionate with one we had considered an enemy; we are forgiving the unforgivable. This voice speaks within us always; all we need is to become quiet enough to hear.

Transformation leads directly to incarnation. Mary is the voice of the heart. She is the teller of stories. She lives compassion. She lives everything. Her voice puts flesh to the Word of God. This is the voice of re-birth, because we live two lives in this world: the life before and the one after the experience of union with God. The Mary voice tells the story of the work of union which is the day to day, moment to moment living with awareness of who and what we are, truly. It is the work of undoing every lie, of every form that does not fit the truth discovered in transformation—the truth of Mother Wisdom which is love and joy.

Living our union with God is what we are here for—living the mysteries, the circle, the spiral that brings to birth Christ's Body. We live Incarnation. Christ Jesus demonstrates that the ultimate or highest state of being goes beyond the bliss of mystical union, beyond the divine fire at the mountaintop, beyond the absorption of the individual self into the one God. The step beyond is to incarnate the mystery of God moment by moment in our daily lives and by so doing to become the Body of Christ.

The end of all our striving is to bring forth in our flesh, as St. Paul intuits and as Mary actually did, the one true God. The incarnation of God, the fulfillment of every divine mystery, the completion of the circle of creation: this is the rosary prayer.

People are creating rosaries out of stones. My sister made hers of malachite. A Baptist woman on the West Coast heard a voice from deep in her heart say "Make rosaries." She didn't even know what a rosary was! Now she's making rosaries from the gem stones given her by the Pacific Ocean. A woman in Vermont and her little girl are making a rosary of rock in their garden. A rock garden rosary! It will be a path, like a sacred labyrinth. They will remember the mysteries of their lives as they tend the flowers and vegetables. Their tending, attending, intending will lead them into the mysteries of God. People who, like me, put their rosaries down years ago, are picking them up once again. They meet in rosary groups. They join prayer circles and the beads dangle from their fingers. They let their fingers touch the beads while they fall asleep at night.

We hardly know what we are doing. It doesn't matter. What we do transforms the world, ourselves, all together. It is one being. Each of us lives every mystery. The beads of the rosary are the sacred moments of our lives. The voices that speak to us from within are voices of healing and transformation. They are voices of joy.

I will buy those lapis beads and make a rosary of my own.

NOTES

[1] I am grateful to Linda Johnsen, author *Daughters of the Goddess: The Women Saints of India,* for helping to clarify Hindu origins of the rosary.

[2] Warner, Marina. *Alone of All Her Sex: The Myth and the Cult of the Virgin Mary.* Alfred A. Knoff. New York: 1976. p. 305.

[3] Walker, Barbara. *The Woman's Encyclopedia of Myths and Secrets.* Harper & Row. San Francisco: 1983. p. 867.

[4] Warner, op. cit. p. 307.

[5] c.f. Ellen M. Umansky, "Creating a Jewish Feminist Theology," in *Weaving the Visions; New Patterns in Feminist Spirituality.* Edited by Judith Plaskow and Carol P. Christ. Harper & Row, San Francisco, 1989, p. 192-193.

[6] Woodruff, Sue. *Meditations with Mechtilde of Magdeburg.* Bear & Co., Inc. Santa Fe, NM. 1982. p. 42.

About the Author

Christin Lore Weber began her spiritual quest on Lake of the Woods in northern Minnesota, a place imprinted on her soul and providing the inspiration for the strong nature imagery found in her writing. When she was still an adolescent she entered a convent where she studied and served for almost fifteen years  and which grounded her in a spiritual practice. After leaving her religious community she continued working to integrate spirituality with everyday life, psychology and theology. She earned a Master of Arts degree in theology and a Doctor of Ministry degree which focused on the connections between psychology and spirituality. She has been a teacher, a lecturer, a spiritual guide, a chaplain in a residential treatment center, and author of six published books and numerous essays.

Christin now lives with her husband, John, in the Pacific Northwest where, she says, "I do common things: walk in the woods and on the beach, make a home, make love, make stories, make rosaries out of stones or glass beads. I never tire of sunlight on the mountains and bay. I try to let everything, every moment, open my heart to the divine call. The quest continues. And I write; I never stop writing."